Cover: Amidst the ruins of Animas Forks stands a once stately and elegant Victorian house. A prominent bay window faces the Animas River. It is generally believed that Thomas F. Walsh, of Camp Bird fame, once owned this house. Contrary to legend, however, his daughter, Evalyn Walsh McLean (an owner of the Hope Diamond), was not born here. Evalyn was born in Denver and it is unlikely she ever lived in Animas Forks. *Photograph by Dave Southworth.*

Ghost Towns and Mining Camps
of the
San Juans

Dave Southworth

Wild Horse Publishing

Cover design by Dave Southworth
Maps by Dave Southworth & United States Geological Survey

Library of Congress Cataloging-in-Publication Data

Southworth, Dave, 1937–
  Ghost Towns and Mining Camps of the San Juans

Bibliography: p. 83
Includes index.
1. Colorado—History 2. Mining Camps—Colorado—History.
3. Frontier and pioneer life—Colorado—History. 4. Cities and towns—Colorado—History.
5. Mines and mineral resources—Colorado—History. 6. Colorado—Description and travel—Guide-books. I. Southworth, Dave II. Title.

ISBN: 1-890778-01-X
Copyright © 1998, 2001 by Wild Horse Publishing.
Printed in the United States of America.

Segments of *Colorado Mining Camps* by Dave Southworth have been used in the composition of *Ghost Towns and Mining Camps of the San Juans*.

Contents

Other Works by Dave Southworth

———————— Books ————————

Colorado Gold Dust: Short Stories and Profiles
Colorado Mining Camps
Gunfighters of the Old West
Feuds on the Western Frontier

———————— Videos ————————

*Colorado Mining Camps: A Pictorial Treasure of the
    Gold and Silver Boom*
Leadville: The Boom Years
Mining Camps of the San Juans
Cripple Creek and the Mining Camps of Teller County
The Mining Camps of Northwest Colorado
The Mining Camps of Gilpin and Clear Creek Counties
The Mining Camps of South Central Colorado
Boulder County Mining Camps: A Look Back

———————— Audio Books ————————

Gunfighters of the Old West

Dave Southworth

Introduction

Ten years after the California Gold Rush, William Green Russell and his party from Georgia discovered gold at Dry Creek in 1858. Hundreds of prospectors, with picks and shovels, flocked to the camps of Denver City and Auraria. The cry was "Pike's Peak or Bust." They broke rocks and ravaged streambeds with little to show for it. Most left in disgust calling the strike a hoax. They were hasty in their decision, however, for gold strikes by George Jackson near Idaho Springs and John Gregory near Central City in the spring of 1859 brought thousands more stampeding into the territory. By summer, over 5,000 men were working the Gregory Lode with more than 100 sluices. Miners were inspired to spread out seeking gold deposits in other parts of the territory. As discoveries were made, towns cropped up throughout the mountains. More immigrants headed west taking with them their hopes, memories, and whatever they could stuff into their wagons.

In February 1861, the Colorado territory was established. The Anglo population of Colorado was set at 25,242 when Governor William Gilpin took the first head count that same year. Men outnumbered women by a margin of thirty to one.

Mining towns popped up as tent cities. Gradually the tents were replaced with log cabins constructed of squared-hewn timber. When a saw mill was completed, frame structures were built, many with tall and massive false fronts. Stores were erected shoulder-to-shoulder so the imposing fronts could hide the buildings behind them. As a town showed signs of permanence, some stone and brick buildings were constructed. Many finer homes were built of Victorian architecture. In certain areas, they were often trimmed with elaborate gingerbread.

The earliest towns had sanitation problems. Much trash was thrown into the streets. Mules, horses, and cattle contributed to the refuse. Personal cleanliness was minimal. Miners worked up a sweat during the daytime, then slept in their clothes, for tent walls were thin and mountain nights were chilly. Many never bothered to bathe, especially during colder weather. As a result, epidemics were common. As families arrived in later migrations most towns became clean and comfortable villages.

Placer mining was most common in the early 1860s. Prospectors scrambled up and down the streams in search of color. When successful, they staked their claims and panned the stream beds. Others combed the mountains in search of exposed ore or float gold. It wasn't long before all of the easily obtainable gold had been found, so miners began tunneling into the mountain sides, sinking shafts to reach their veins. Gold found in this manner was difficult to extract from the ore. Prof. Nathaniel Hill solved the ore reduction problem when he constructed his Boston and Colorado Smelter in Black Hawk in 1868.

Prospectors pushed deeper into the mountains discovering new mining areas. During the seventies and eighties, mining really boomed. When silver was discovered in Leadville in 1877—the year after Colorado achieved statehood

—the population of Lake County grew from a handful to nearly twenty-four thousand. In a few short months, silver became more dominant than gold throughout the state.

For years the Ute Indians who roamed the mountains of Colorado remained friendly with white settlers. Their patience was stretched, however, as more prospectors moved into the mountains in search of new mining areas. The United States government made several agreements with Chief Ouray which resulted in a reduction of their territory. During an uprising at the White River Ute Indian Agency in 1879, a band of Utes killed Nathan Meeker, an Indian agent, in what became known as the Meeker Massacre. As a result, the tribe was relocated further west, predominately into Utah, virtually giving white settlers a reign over all of Colorado.

The population explosion in the mining towns was abetted by a maze of railroads which snaked through valleys and over mountains bringing supplies and more people. The railroads also provided a means of shipping ore from the mines to the smelters with a lot less hardship.

As mining moved deeper beneath the surface of the earth, more capital was required. Mining companies, capitalized in the east or even in Europe, pumped money into mining operations. Corporate organization of lucrative claims occurred. In many instances, the original claim holder became an employee of the corporation. Hydraulic mining became popular in certain areas.

Repeal of the Sherman Silver Purchase Act in 1893 created a devaluation of silver and dealt a devastating blow to the mining industry. Many mines were shutdown, communities became ghost towns, and railroads were abandoned. Although the bonanza had not yet occurred in the Cripple Creek-Victor area, gold production throughout much of the state was declining by this time also. The remains of mines, old buildings, and ghost towns bring back the days of yesteryear —a colorful page in Colorado history.

Technically a ghost town is one which is not inhabited. For the most part, the towns which are uninhabited are the ones which are in various stages of collapse. Some of those which have withstood the test of time have had a resurgence. Conversely, there are many cities and towns which played an important part in the mining boom that have been inhabited continually since they were established.

It is said that a picture is worth a thousand words. Naturally it depends on the picture. Sometimes it is easiest to depict the hustle and bustle of a roaring mining town with an old photograph. On the other hand, switching from past to present, a photo of a few scattered logs or an empty site is a waste of space when a few words may best describe that a town has weathered into oblivion. Photographs have been selected to portray "then" and "now" as proficiently as possible.

Each site may be located by using the geographical description (and directions) in conjunction with the proper map. U.S. Forest Service maps offer more detail of any area. When seeking a remote site, it might be helpful to travel with a topographic map and compass.

Many mining camps are accessible by automobile. Others may be reached with a 4-wheel drive vehicle. An experienced mountain trail horse, trail bike, or a back-pack hike is recommended travel to a couple of locations. This can be great fun, but it's not for everybody. If such a trek is a hardship, much may not have been missed, for some of these remote sites are in high country where heavy snows over the years have barely left traces of once active mining camps.

It is necessary to cross a labyrinth of jeep trails and pack trails to reach some destinations. In cases like this it is wise to get very specific directions or take a guide. Guides, outfitters, and jeep tours are generally expensive. Most are reputable and interesting. Caution is advised before making any trip, however, because some tours will literally "take you for a ride." Find out in advance exactly where the tour goes, what will actually be seen, how long it will take, and the cost.

Mines, mining towns, and spectacular scenery certainly go together. Colorado is rich in minerals and rich in pastoral splendor. Most of the mining towns are (or were) located in places of great beauty. No place is this more evident than in the awesome mountains and luscious valleys of the San Juans.

Dave Southworth

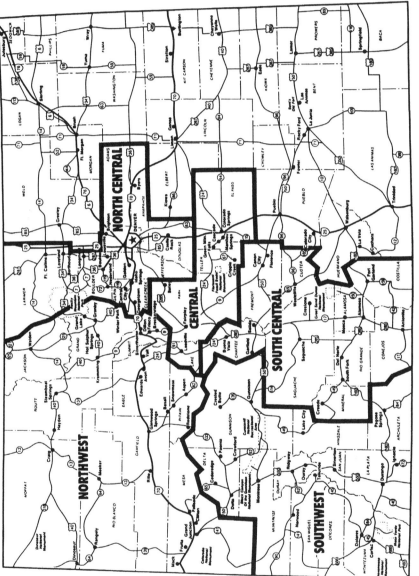

STATE OF COLORADO

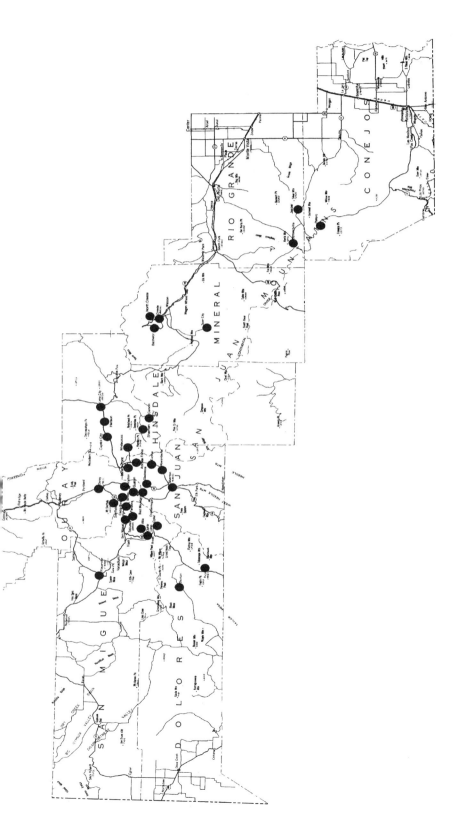

SAN JUAN MOUNTAIN REGION

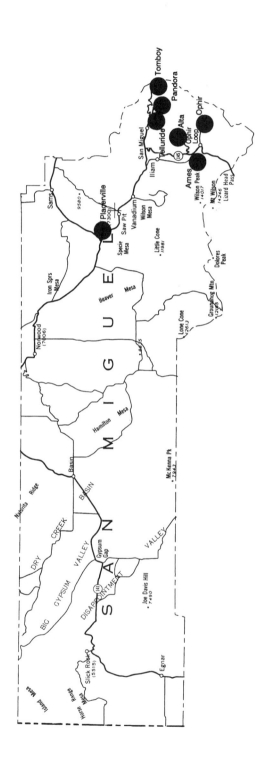

SAN MIGUEL COUNTY

• •

TELLURIDE

Location: 41 miles south of Ridgway via State Highways 62 and 145

Telluride is experiencing dramatic expansion as a year-round resort. The town itself, which is nestled on the floor of a gorgeous and spectacular box canyon, looks much as it did a century ago—with Victorian homes laced with gingerbread and topped with tin roofs. The scenic hills above, however, are in the midst of exciting development. Telluride has become a playground for many movie stars and other celebrities, and some have built beautiful homes in the area. As new resorts pop their heads above the treetops, the future looks very bright indeed.

It all began when John Fallon discovered the Sheridan vein ten miles east of Telluride, in August of 1875. The lode was tapped by other claims—the Union, Mendota, and Smuggler. The Smuggler was the result of a brilliant deduction by J. B. Ingram. Ingram thought that both the Sheridan and Union claims seemed too large. He discovered that both exceeded their legal allowance by several hundred feet. So, he staked the Smuggler on the area covered by the excess. The best producing mines during the '80s were the Smuggler, Mendota, Union, Argentine, Cleveland, Cimarron, Sheridan, Hidden Treasure, and Bullion. Following mergers and purchases, the Smuggler-Union emerged as the area's biggest producer. By the turn of the century, the company had 35 miles of tunnels. By that time, the Liberty Bell and the Tomboy had also emerged as top producers as well. Near the site of the Tomboy, the Japan and Columbia were located in 1894. In later years, several properties were purchased by the Idarado Mining Company. With advanced milling methods, Idarado became the largest producer of all.

During the late '70s, several small camps cropped up in the canyon along the San Miguel River. San Miguel City was the largest at first, but Columbia was closer to the mines and soon outdistanced all of the other camps. In 1881 the name was changed from Columbia to Telluride. Although its location was rather isolated, Telluride's growth was steady through the 1880s. The community, and the mining industry on which its economy was reliant, received a real boost with the arrival of the railroad in 1890.

Although Telluride was most noted for its lawlessness, it had another side also. To occupy the leisure time of those so inclined, there were many civic clubs, fraternal organizations, dances, and concerts. Ethnic groups had their own meeting places such as Swedish Hall and Finn Hall. Much advance preparation was made each year for the huge Fourth of July celebration. Fireworks, a huge parade, and a grand ball highlighted the festivities.

Whoever referred to Telluride with a play on words, "To hell you ride!", wasn't far wrong. According to historian Frank Hall, there were always "more than a sufficiency of saloons" in Telluride. Gambling dens such as Pacific Hall were quick to fleece a miner of his hard-earned wages—so were the brothels. Parlor houses were important in most all predominantly male mining towns, and Telluride was no exception. Its "sporting" establishments ranged from the Pick and Gad, a popular bordello, down to the simple cribs. A man with many enemies was the town marshal, Jim Clark. He was a crack shot who carried two pistols and stashed rifles at strategic locations around town in case he needed one in a hurry. In return for favors from storekeepers, Clark would bully debtors into paying their bills. While walking his beat one night, a shot rang out from the darkness between two stores and killed him instantly. Nobody knew who fired the shot—and, nobody really cared. In broad daylight one afternoon in 1889, with the help of two sidekicks, Butch Cassidy robbed his first bank in Telluride. The biggest bank heist, however, occurred years later and was an inside job. Following the crash of 1929 many banks failed. When Charles Waggoner, president of the Bank of Telluride, couldn't cover the deposits of his Telluride friends, he felt as though he had to do something quickly. By using certain banking codes, he had large drafts deposited by top New York banks to the credit of his bank. He covered the deposits of his Telluride friends, and in an effort to hide the rest of the money he scattered it across the country in smaller deposits. The fraud totalled a half million dollars. Waggoner was arrested and imprisoned, but to the people of Telluride he was a hero.

Much of the violence which occurred in Telluride was a result of the labor war. The Western Federation of Miners called a strike at the Smuggler-Union on May 2, 1901, to protest wages based on quantity of ore mined rather than the standard three dollar rate for eight hours which was common throughout most of the state. After six weeks of inactivity, mine owners hired nonunion "scabs" at wages of three dollars per day, and reopened the mines. A confrontation occurred between 250 armed and irate union workers and the nonunion men. After three men were killed and six more injured, the scabs were run out of town. The strike was settled and the union had won the first round. The mine owners won the second round, however, and they won it big. Tomboy miners struck in September of 1903 when the new mill was opened with nonunion workers. Faced with a new threat of impending violence, Governor James Peabody declared a state of martial law. The militia seized control. Union laborers and union sympathizers were loaded in rail cars and run out of town. Many were beaten first. A statement was issued by the mine owners: "...We do not recognize a union in Telluride. There is no strike in Telluride. There is nothing to settle."

Every winter there existed the threat of snowslides. A series of disastrous slides started in March of 1902. One hit the Liberty Bell sweeping away the aerial tramway and several men. A second slide buried a rescue party which was searching for bodies. The following day another drift forced a new group of rescuers to return to town. Meanwhile, a Cornish miner started the trek from ten miles east of Telluride to join the rescue effort. He was also buried by a snowslide. No bodies were uncovered for some time and it was months before the Cornish miner was found. Telluride was devastated by the chain of events.

The mines above Telluride produced gold, silver, copper, zinc and other minerals. For several years, silver was the backbone of Telluride's economy. Following the silver crash in 1893, the mining industry turned its attention to gold. Today, the economy thrives on tourism—and indeed its future is bright.

● ●

PLACERVILLE

Location: 17 miles northwest of Telluride on State Highway 145

West of the Dallas Divide, along the San Miguel River, Colonel S. H. Baker and his group of prospectors discovered placer gold in 1876. A tent colony sprang up which was originally called Dry Diggings, then Hang Town. The following year its name was changed to Placerville. The Lower San Miguel Mining District was established as well.

The town of Placerville was platted in 1877. The original townsite was located at the intersection of present-day State Highway 62 and State Highway 145. Less than one half mile southeast of town, a general store and saloon were constructed on "Smith's Ranch" in 1879, and lots were sold. Through all of the '80s Placerville consisted of two sites. By 1890, when the Denver & Rio Grande Southern Railroad arrived at Placerville, most of the townsite had shifted, and the original location was soon to vanish.

The Bennett Dry Placer Amalgamator began operating in 1881. During the '80s the Keokuk Hydraulic Mining Company washed down an entire hill near Placerville. They maintained offices in the community, as did the St. Louis and San Miguel Company and the Mount Wilson Placer Mining Company.

As mining diminished, livestock became the backbone of Placerville. The Philadelphia Cattle Company established offices in town. As was the case in much of the old west, sheep herders and cattle ranchers didn't mix too well. On one occasion several sheepmen were killed in a range war. Ultimately Placerville became an important railroad shipping point for both cattle and sheep.

● ●

OPHIR

Location: 14 miles south of Telluride via State Highway 145 and the Ophir Pass Road

Two miles east of State Highway 145 at the foot of Ophir Pass, lies the town of Ophir. At one time the town was called Old Ophir to avoid confusion with the community located at the Ophir Loop, two miles west—originally known as Howard's Fork, and later Ophir. If that's not confusing enough, the Ophir Station was also located at the loop, and the small community located there was sometimes referred to by that name.

Although there are other versions for the name's origin, Ophir was probably named for the biblical site where gold was discovered at King Solomon's Mine.

Lt. Howard, for whom Howard's Fork is named, made the first strike in the area in 1875. Many others followed. The north face of Yellow Mountain was where it all started. The Butterfly-Terrible, Silver Bell, Caribbean, Nevada, and the Badger were among the more profitable mines. And, they produced constantly right through the turn of the century.

Ophir (Old Ophir) had a population of about 400 at its peak. By the late 1890's the town had a water works, electricity, a hotel, a stamp mill, churches, and a school house—although a future school master was runoff for failing to join the miner's union.

Otto Mears was a road-builder and railroad builder who didn't know the word "impossible." The Ophir Loop was one of his crowning achievements. The major construction project enabled the railroad to run from Telluride to Durango. Three tiers of tracks with loops crossing above and below each other and trestles sometimes one hundred feet high were the result of Mears' challenge. Depending upon how they reacted, passengers were either thrilled or chilled by the experience.

The history of Ophir and Ophir Pass is sprinkled with tragedy—mostly due to the harsh winters and destructive avalanches. A story often told is that of Swedish mailman, Sven Nilson, who carried the mail back and forth from Silverton to Ophir throughout the year, even in the most hazardous weather. In fact, the winter trek over the pass was so dangerous he was paid a salary more than double that of the average miner. In December of 1883, Nilson left Silverton during a blizzard carrying Ophir's Christmas mail. He never reached Ophir. Several searchers combed the area, but to no avail. More than a year and a half later, Nilson's body was found in a ravine—with the pouch carrying Ophir's Christmas mail still strapped to his back.

The population of Ophir gradually declined after the turn of the century, until it had become a ghost town by the 1920s. Today there has been a revitalization of Ophir, and the town is once again inhabited—mostly with summer residents.

● ●

ALTA

Location: South of Telluride; 5 miles east of State Highway 145 on the road to Alta Lakes

The Alta Mine was discovered in 1878, and about a mile away a cluster of cabins were built which became the town of Alta. The following year, in 1879, the famous Gold King Mine was located. The Gold King was a rich mine, but expensive to operate until L. L. Nunn brought in electrical power (see Ames).

The history of Alta followed that of the mines. During periods when they were closed, the town was virtually empty. The Gold King Mine worked more often than not, and did so through World War II.

Alta, which is situated in a very picturesque location, was never very large. In fact it never had a church or post office. However, it did have a school, a large boardinghouse, several mining buildings, an aerial tram, and many cabins. The entrance to the Black Hawk Tunnel is at Alta. It's 9,000 feet of passages reach both the Alta and St. Louis veins.

In 1945, a tragic incident occurred at the last of Alta's three mills. A fire raged while seven men were beneath the earth's surface. The superintendent ordered the portal dynamited in order to cut off the draft which was feeding the fire. One of the men sealed underground was the superintendent's son.

Due to the longevity of the Gold King Mine, Alta became a ghost town later than most. As a result, many deteriorating buildings still stand.

● ○ ●

AMES

Location: 15 miles south of Telluride via State Highway 145, near Ophir

The town of Ames sprang to life in 1882 when a smelter was constructed by the San Miguel River. Because of poor planning, the life of the smelting works was short lived. The San Miguel River ran through a deep canyon. Transporting ores into the canyon for smelting was an expensive proposition. Other smelters were built at more geographically feasible locations. When the smelter at Ames closed most of the town packed up and moved on.

It wasn't long before Ames experienced a revival. The Gold King Mine at Alta was experiencing difficulties because of its great costs of operating at such a high altitude—12,000 feet. The Gold King and the town of Ames were saved by the visionary genius of L. L. Nunn, the mine's attorney.

Nunn envisioned building an electrical plant at Ames which would harness the power of the San Miguel River, then transmit it up to the Gold King Mine. Many scoffed at the idea but the plant was built anyway. It worked—fuel costs were cut and expenses were trimmed—the Gold King was saved. The result was the first commercial transmission of high-pressure electricity in history.

The success of the endeavor prompted Nunn to build high-tension lines across Imogene Pass (elevation: 13,000 feet) to serve Camp Bird and other mines on the Ouray side of the range.

● ●

● ●

PANDORA

Location: 1 mile east of Telluride

Below spectacular Bridal Veil Falls with its water cascading 365 feet down the cliffside, in an area once called Water Fall Gulch, lies the site of Pandora. Initially there were two small camps called Folsome and Newport at this location. Folsome preceded Newport, which was the original name of Pandora. The two little camps grew together to form the settlement which was named in 1881 for the Pandora Mine. The old Imogene Pass Road (which has been closed for years) originally ascended from Pandora across to Camp Bird.

The Smuggler-Union Mill was the main source of livelihood for the residents of Pandora. Aerial trams carted ore from the Smuggler and Union mines, high on the hill above town, down to the mill for processing. The Smuggler-Union had a history of labor strike and violence. In 1902, mine manager Arthur Collins was assassinated while sitting in his Pandora home. His replacement, B. Wells, narrowly escaped death when a bomb beneath his bed exploded and destroyed the house. Both the assassination and attempted assassination were blamed on the Western Federation of Miners Union.

Today the Smuggler-Union and Liberty Bell properties and the site of Pandora are all on property owned by the Idarado Mining Company. The Idarado is removing tailings and cleaning up the area. The trailer park at Pandora is also being removed. By the year 2011, law will allow development of this property which by then should be prime real estate.

● ●

TOMBOY

Location: 5 miles east of Telluride via Forest Route 869 (Tomboy Road)

Otis C. Thomas located the Tomboy Mine in 1880 on Savage Fork, high above Telluride. Tomboy was Thomas' nickname, but the claim was staked for George Rohwer. Because of its rather inaccessible location, there was very little activity in the area for several years.

Following the silver crash of 1893 many miners turned their attention to gold. Suddenly the Tomboy Gold Mines Company began producing handsomely. The small settlement of Savage Basin Camp blossomed to a population of about 900, and was renamed Tomboy.

Tomboy was very reliant upon Telluride as a supply center but it didn't have to rely on Telluride for "pleasure." Midway between Tomboy and the Smuggler Mine was a red-light district called "The Jungle"—a mixture of brothels, poker dens, and saloons.

Mine owners tried valiantly to clean up the area, but without much luck.

As with most camps that were adjacent to successful mines, Tomboy's history followed that of the Tomboy Mine and other mining properties in the vicinity. In 1894 other rich strikes were made nearby—the Columbia and the Japan. The Rothchilds of London purchased the Tomboy in 1897 for $2,000,000. The high mountain camp (which is located over 2,600 feet in elevation above Telluride) was booming. Mining operations declined after the turn of the century. The Tomboy Mine closed in 1927.

The remains of Tomboy are rapidly deteriorating, but there is still much to see. A trip to the old townsite is enriched with spectacular scenery.

● ●

Ox teams pull covered wagons of supplies down the main street of early Telluride. *Archives, University of Colorado at Boulder.*

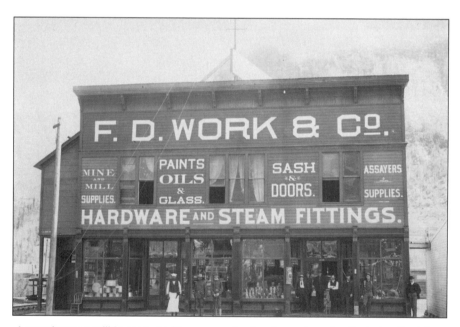

A storekeeper, militia men, and townspeople stand on a boardwalk during the labor strike at Telluride in 1903. *Denver Public Library, Western History Department.*

Telluride, as it looks today. *Dave Southworth.*

St. Patrick's Catholic Church at Telluride was established in 1896. *Dave Southworth.*

The community of Placerville in October 1887.
Denver Public Library, Western History Department.

Looking down the main street of Ophir in August 1883. *Colorado Historical Society.*

The boardinghouse at Alta. *Dave Southworth.*

Alta, inside looking out. *Dave Southworth.*

The community of Pandora. Smuggler-Union's mill is in the foreground. *Denver Public Library, Western History Department.*

The Tomboy Gold Mines Company at Marshall Basin above Telluride. *Colorado Historical Society.*

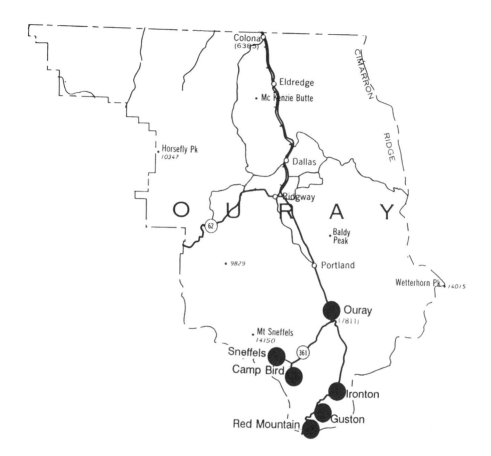

Colona
(638?)

Eldredge

Mc Kenzie Butte

CIMARRON

RIDGE

Horsefly Pk
10347

Dallas

O U R A Y

Ridgway

62

Baldy
Peak

• 9829

Portland

Wetterhorn Pk 14015

Ouray
(7811)

Mt Sneffels
14150

Sneffels

361

Camp Bird

Ironton

Red Mountain

Guston

OURAY COUNTY

●●●

OURAY

Location: 37 miles south of Montrose, or 23 miles north of Silverton, on U. S. Highway 550

Ouray is located at the bottom of a bowl of steep cliffs which drop below the jagged, snow-capped peaks of the Uncompahgre Mountains. The valley is stark—yet spectacular and beautiful.

In 1875 A. J. Staley and Logan Whitlock, while fishing along the Uncompahgre River at the mouth of Canyon Creek, discovered the Trout and Fisherman lodes. During the same year, A. W. Begole and Jack Eckles located the Cedar, Clipper, and Mineral Farm lodes—and the rush was on.

A town was platted which was first called Uncompahgre City, then renamed Ouray. Through his unparalleled strength of character and artful negotiations, Chief Ouray of the Utes was more responsible than any other person for gaining peace between the Indian and white man in Colorado. It is fitting that the city of Ouray is named in his honor.

Printing presses were carried over the mountains by wagon train, and the first newspaper was established in 1877—the *Ouray Times* (later named the *Plaindealer*). Shortly thereafter a second newspaper began operations—the *San Juan Sentinel*. The third, and most famous newspaper appeared in September 1879. The opinionated and controversial *Solid Muldoon* of David Frakes Day was a widely quoted publication. By this same year the population of Ouray was approaching 1,000. There were three hotels, three churches, several stores, saloons, gambling dens, and a "red light" district which was located at the north edge of town.

W. J. Benton's Star Saloon was the first frame building constructed in town. When Ouray became county seat, the saloon was converted into the courthouse. The bar was removed and the first floor became the city hall. The rooms on the second floor, which were once sleeping quarters, were changed into county offices.

The only known lynching of a woman in Colorado mining camp history occurred in Ouray. In 1884, after a man and woman had been jailed for allegedly raping and killing a 10 year old orphan girl, an irate mob of citizens dragged the couple from jail and hanged them.

Mrs. Dixon operated one of the earliest boardinghouses. In actuality it was a cabin without much room. Guests brought their own bedrolls and slept under the tables where Mrs. Dixon served meals. She did well and saved her money, then built a fine hotel—the Dixon House.

Transportation was a major problem during the early years, and remained so until the arrival of master road builder Otto Mears in 1881. Increased access boosted Ouray and its economy. Within a few years the railroad arrived (in 1887), advancing the community even more.

Snowslides and bitter winters were also a problem during the early history of the mining district. On one occasion a mining accident injured two workers at the Terrible. While en route to the location of the accident, four rescuers were killed in an avalanche. Seven miners and twenty-seven horses and mules lost their lives in another slide. Later, the disastrous blizzards during the winter of 1905-06 claimed many lives. On the lighter side, a story is told of a man who was buried in a mine by a snowdrift. He tunneled his way out and walked into Ouray two days later, only to find his name in the obituaries.

In addition to the aforementioned mines, some of the better producers were the American Nettie, the Virginius, Chief Ouray, the Bachelor, Wedge, Khedive, Calliope, and the Banner American. The silver crash of 1893 made a dent in the economy, but Ouray wouldn't crumble. Whereas the highest percentage of mining had been silver, the district turned its attention to gold and other minerals.

The Bachelor Mine is an example of how faith, hard work, and perseverance paid off. The owners were a cook, a mail carrier, and a prospector. They put all of their earnings back into the mine. After tunneling 700 feet they cut a gold vein and their prayers were answered. The Bachelor Mine produced about $30,000 per month.

By the 1890s much of downtown Ouray had been rebuilt in stone and brick —such as the elegant Beaumont Hotel, at the corner of Main and Fifth Streets. Its stately architecture and luxurious interior made it the finest hostelry in the Uncompahgres. The railroad brought more people, so consequently there were more gambling dens and parlor houses. The number of saloons had increased to thirty. In 1890 the population of Ouray County was 6,510. Following the repeal of the Sherman Silver Purchase Act, the population dwindled to 4,731 in 1900. Generally, there was a continuing decline until 1940 when the population had dropped to 2,089, at which point it stabilized. Fifty years later, in 1990, the population was 2,295. Picturesque Ouray has continued to be a popular spot for summer tourists.

● ●

SNEFFELS

Location: 6 miles southwest of Ouray via State Highway 361

The Wheel of Fortune, Yankee Boy, and Virginius mines were among the earliest discoveries near Sneffels—and the little camp became a lively place. Additional discoveries followed, such as the Ruby Trust, Hidden Treasure, Humboldt, Governor, and the Senator. A fine producer was the Atlas, which like several others, had a mill and boardinghouse. The mines of Mount Sneffels yielded an estimated $27,000,000 during the boom years. Some of the ore assayed as high as $40,000 per ton. Mount Sneffels (as well as the settlement) was named for Jules Verne's Icelandic peak in *A Journey to the Center of the Earth*.

Sneffels was both a gold and silver camp. The silver came easy, but gold was only encountered after shafts were driven very deep into the mountain side. In 1884 the Revenue Tunnel was constructed to intercept the rich Virginius. The bore was made at a point nearly 3,000 feet in elevation below the mouth of the original shaft then extended about three miles into the mountain. The project, which was financed by the Thatcher brothers of Ouray, cost $600,000 but paid for itself almost immediately. The tunnel not only solved water and ventilation problems but opened up enough new ore to keep the mills running for years to come. The property became known as the Revenue-Virginius, employed 600, and developed into one of the best mines in Colorado.

The road from Ouray to Sneffels is steep, narrow in places, and partially a shelf notched in the mountain side. At one time the road was a continuous traffic jam, with packed trains, freight wagons, loggers, stagecoaches, and individuals walking or on horseback. The road was treacherous during winters and the result was many accidents. There is much less traffic today. Along it's route, and from Mount Sneffels above, the scenery is spectacular.

• •

RED MOUNTAIN

Location: 13 miles south of Ouray on U.S. Highway 550

A few claims were staked in the vicinity of Red Mountain as early as 1879, but nothing much happened until late 1882. A large cavern was discovered which glittered from the rich lead carbonate lining the walls. The find was dubbed the National Belle. For fear they would miss out if they waited until spring, prospectors flocked to Red Mountain in the dead of winter.

The ground was frozen, and proper foundations couldn't be built. Nonetheless, several mining camps popped up before the snow thawed, and others followed on both sides of Red Mountain Pass. The community now generally called Red Mountain was once known as Red Mountain Town, and was the largest of the lucrative camps in the Red Mountain District. Guston and Ironton were substantial towns to the north. Additionally, Yankee Girl was a small camp adjacent to the Yankee Girl Mine near Guston. South of the summit were short-lived Red Mountain City and Sheridan Junction (Chattanooga).

Red Mountain (Red Mountain Town) became the largest and the most prosperous in the district. The camp which began in January 1883, was a boom town in two short months. In March 1883 the *Solid Muldoon* (Ouray) stated: "Five weeks ago the site where Red Mountain now stands was woodland mesa, covered with heavy spruce timber. Today, hotels, printing offices, groceries, meat markets, ... a telephone office, saloons, dance houses are up and booming; the blast is heard on every side and prospectors can be seen snowshoeing in every direction." Initially, Red Mountain was accessible from several directions

—and all were dangerous trails. The difficult access was solved by road builder Otto Mears. After the "Grandest Highway in the Rockies" was surveyed, Red Mountain residents began to scramble for lots in the flat close to the highway site. Mears' road—generally the predecessor of the Million Dollar Highway —was constructed north from Silverton through Red Mountain and on to Ouray. The whole town moved about a half-mile in order to be close to the toll road.

The road was not enough, however, so Otto Mears built a railroad which connected with the Denver & Rio Grande at Silverton then snaked through the mountains to the north for twenty miles. The "Rainbow Route" as it was dubbed, arrived into Red Mountain in September 1888 amid much fanfare.

During the boom years saloons and gambling halls never closed—day or night. Violence was commonplace. A Saturday rarely passed that didn't end up in some kind of brawl. The lively community also had other forms of entertainment. Dances, plays, concerts, and sporting events were held on a regular basis, and were attended by guests from as far away as Ouray and Silverton.

In addition to the aforementioned National Belle Mine, there were many other top producers. The Yankee Girl (see Guston) topped them all—producing over $8,000,000. Three of the earliest finds were the Congress, the Summit, and the Enterprise. Population estimates during the boom years range from 1,000 to about 10,000. It is more likely that the latter figure included the whole mining district, with about 3,000 in the town of Red Mountain. Once the prospecting frenzy passed and everyone settled in to work the established mines, the population was closer to the 1,000 estimate. Following the demonetization of silver in 1893, the population dropped to 400 and continued to decline. The population by 1896 was 40. Off and on again mining continued through the ensuing years, but all of the camps in the Red Mountain Mining District died long ago.

● ●

IRONTON

Location: 8 miles south of Ouray on U.S. Highway 550

Ironton is another town that blossomed during the Red Mountain mining craze. The town began in January 1883 when snow was cleared and 300 tents pitched. The camp initially had two names—Ironton and Copper Glen, the latter which was quickly dropped.

The American Girl, Cora Belle, Mountain King, Silver Bell and the Lost Day were all mines that produced well. Much of the economy and livelihood of the community, however, was due to the enormous success of the Yankee Girl Mine at nearby Guston. Even though Ironton had ten saloons, it grew with an element of refinement and class. Merchants of some of the better stores in Ouray and Silverton opened branches at Ironton. People from Red Mountain and Guston often shopped at Ironton's specialty shops. The town emerged as a supply center for the region. It also was important as a transportation center and stopover for stagecoach lines (such as the Ouray Stage and Bus Co.) and supply wagons.

Arrival of the railroad into Ironton boasted activity even more. A grand celebration welcomed the first train in November 1888. The rails of Otto Mears' Rainbow Route left Silverton and climbed across Red Mountain Pass at an elevation of 11,650 feet, then descended to Ironton. Upwards of 20,000 tons of ore were transported out of the Red Mountain District by train annually.

Ironton never had a major conflagration—possibly because it was well equipped. There was a firehouse and hose company, and fire hydrants were scattered throughout the town. Not only were the waterworks impressive, but Ironton also had an electric light plant.

The silver crash of 1893 closed most of Ironton's mines. People moved on in search of greener pastures. A new, but brief, boom occurred when gold was discovered in 1898. Ironton remained inhabited into the early 1930s. Outside of Ironton proper stood a cabin nestled in a nearby grove of aspens where a recluse named Larson lived on for another three decades.

●●●

GUSTON

Location: 11 miles south of Ouray on U.S. Highway 550

John Robinson had much to do with four of the earliest discoveries in the vicinity. During the summer of 1881, Robinson and his group of prospectors staked the Guston claim. At the time, it yielded low-grade ore and the project was nearly abandoned. The following year, he discovered nearly pure galena about 300 yards from the Guston and staked the Yankee Girl. Further digging at the Yankee Girl didn't yield much either, and Robinson's operating capital was running low. He knew the mine had promise, however, and staked claims on opposite sides which he named the Robinson and Orphan Boy. He then sold the Yankee Girl to a partnership for $125,000 providing the capital he needed. The Yankee Girl sputtered for its new owners as well—but when it hit, it was a bonanza. Its production exceeded 25% of the entire district—yielding over $8,000,000. The Guston, Robinson and Orphan Boy were also successful endeavors. Other good mines at Guston were the Saratoga, Candice, Paymaster and the Genesee-Vanderbilt.

Guston was a small town, with a population of about 300, yet it had the distinction of having the only church in the entire Red Mountain Mining District. In 1891, the Rev. William Davis was sent by the Congregational Church to Red Mountain in order to establish a mission. The pastor received a polite but cool reception. Finding no place in which to conduct worship services, he went to Guston where he was cordially received. More determined than ever, Davis set out to raise money for construction of a church. Contributions were received from Silverton to Ouray, the land and pews were donated, and the little church became a reality. Somebody suggested that a mine whistle should be installed in the belfry in order to be heard near and far. And so it was. It is the only church known to have announced its services with the shrill blast of a whistle.

● ●

CAMP BIRD

Location: 5 miles southwest of Ouray via State Highway 361

Flamboyant Evalyn Walsh McLean wrote a book entitled *Father Struck It Rich*, in which she tells the story of Thomas Walsh and the Camp Bird Mine. Walsh was an Irishman and a carpenter by trade. Bridge building brought him to Colorado. His burning desire to get rich quick turned him to prospecting. In 1896 Walsh discovered gold—very rich gold—in Imogene Basin high above Ouray. He immediately purchased approximately 100 claims in the area and consolidated them under the name of Camp Bird. It wasn't long before his mining property produced over $1,000,000 per year, and it eventually became the second largest producer in Colorado (only the Portland Mine near Cripple Creek was larger).

When Evalyn married Edward B. McLean, whose family owned the *Washington Post*, the newlyweds received $100,000 from each family as a wedding gift. Later Evalyn purchased the famous Hope Diamond which she dangled in front of Washington and Denver society.

For his employees Walsh built a posh boardinghouses. The facilities which accommodated 400 men had marble-topped lavatories, electric lights, steam heat, china plates, and even a piano. Meals were often served that rivaled the finest restaurants.

Walsh was already a multimillionaire when he sold the Camp Bird properties, in May 1902, to an English syndicate for 3.5 million dollars in cash, a half-million in shares of stock, and royalties on future profits. To show his gratitude, the generous Thomas Walsh gave employees bonus checks of up to $5,000. Before his death in 1910, he had received 6 million dollars from the sale of the Camp Bird.

Each winter snow was always a problem for the high-mountain community. Through the years snowslides killed several men. Geographically, the site is reached via narrow, winding mountain roads. It was even necessary to construct a two-mile long aerial tramway from the mines to the mill. Camp Bird produced well however—and continued to produce.

● ●

Ouray about 1886. The Beaumont Hotel (at right center)
is under construction. *Colorado Historical Society.*

Ouray's Holt & Foster Building houses the
Western Hotel and Restaurant. *Dave Southworth.*

Sneffels at the turn of the century. *Denver Public Library, Western History Department.*

Looking down on Red Mountain Town in 1888. *Denver Public Library, Western History Department.*

The "Rainbow Route" of Otto Mears arrives at Red Mountain Town in September 1888. *Denver Public Library, Western History Department.*

The Joker Tunnel Boardinghouse near Red Mountain. *Dave Southworth.*

Ironton in 1888 as seen from a nearby mountainside. *Colorado Historical Society.*

Ironton is totally deserted. *Dave Southworth.*

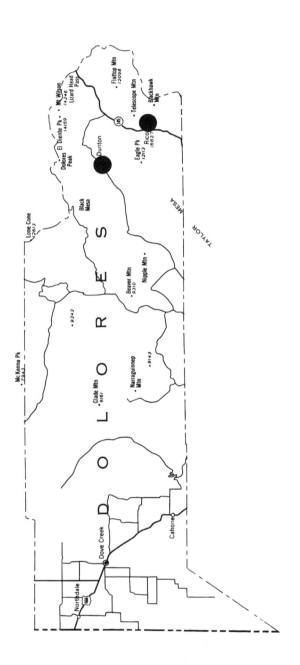

DOLORES COUNTY

• •

RICO

Location: 37 miles northeast of Dolores on State Highway 145

A rich strike was made here in July 1869 by a prospecting party from Santa Fe. The group was comprised of Joe Fearheller, William Hill, Jack Eccles, Tom Sager, "Tinker" Brown, "Pony" Whitmore, and a fellow named Miller. Several other strikes followed. Of the early mines, the Atlantic Cable and the Dolores (later to become the Aztec) were the most productive.

Although a smelting furnace was constructed in 1870, the camp remained a tent colony for several years just waiting for something to happen—and then it did. Senator John P. Jones and other Nevada investors purchased several lodes for $60,000 during the summer of 1879. The mill-sites were surveyed into lots. During the month of August alone, the first 105 log cabins were constructed within the community which was newly named Rico (Spanish for rich). The fall season of 1879 brought many other "firsts" to Rico. A fellow named "Frenchy" was murdered by "Kid" McGoldrick, resulting in Rico's first burial. McGoldrick was sentenced to six years which he never served. The first sermon was preached by Rev. H. P. Roberts of Silverton. After the sermon a large purse was collected for a horse race at the newly established Dolores Jockey Club, and everyone adjourned to the track. A postal route was established, an Episcopal church organized, and Rico had its first dance. The Thanksgiving Day Ball was held at Theodore Barlow's store. Eight ladies attended.

Though Rico had several saloons and was relatively wild, it also had its element of culture. In 1880 the Literary Society was formed. A school was also established with Miss Alice Snyder as its teacher.

There was a food shortage and a bread famine during the winter of '79-80. When John Foote's pack train arrived in the spring, he sold hundred pound sacks of flour for $35. With his new wealth, Foote built a dance hall which entertained a thousand visitors at its grand opening.

In January 1891, the first issue of *The Rico Democrat* advised, "The high grade mines, foremost among which are the Enterprise, Jumbo, C. H. C., Montezuma, Cobbler, and Newman Group, have had a steady output during the year past." More producing mines were the Golden Age, Aspen, Nebraska, Vestal, General Logan, Amazon, Stanley, Butler, Snow Flake and many others. The Enterprise was located and modestly operated by David Swickhimer. Operating capital was acquired when Laura, his wife, won $5,000 on a lottery ticket. The mine developed into a top silver producer. David Swickhimer was elected sheriff in November 1883 and later owned a saloon which was locally known as "Swick's Place." He sold the mine in 1891 for $1.25 million dollars and became president of the Rico State Bank.

When the railroad of Otto Mears arrived in 1891, there was a celebration that lasted for days. The ensuing boom was greater than anything Rico had seen in the past. By 1892 the city had a population of 5,000. There were two newspapers, many stores and hotels, 23 saloons, and a red light district which was three blocks long. The city was named county seat, and the attractive brick Dolores County courthouse was constructed.

The following article appeared November 21, 1891, in *The Rico Weekly Sun.* It might be representative of the male mind-set in Rico at the time. The article should be self explanatory—well, possibly. It read as follows:

"Rico may not be able to compete with neighboring towns in wrestling, or distant states in rock drilling, but we're well up on low-grade ore shipments, waltz quadrilles and beautiful women. Call at the *Sun* office and see our galaxy of female loveliness. The constellation embraces everything from carrot-tinted blondes to buxom brunettes."

The devaluation of silver in 1893 dealt Rico a severe blow. Many businesses closed and the population quickly dropped below 1,000.

The area mines have produced many minerals—and have continued to do so through the twentieth century. Although only a shadow of the old community, Rico endures today. During renovation in 1992 on the old Catholic Church (once the schoolhouse) the original old blackboards were uncovered.

● ●

DUNTON

Location: 10 miles west of State Highway 145, or 36 miles northeast of Dolores

Dunton sprang into existence in 1885 with the discovery of the Emma Mine. As other claims were established along the West Dolores River, the town blossomed. Dunton was a lively place with plenty of saloons to serve its nearly all-male population of three hundred.

According to legend, the infamous Butch Cassidy fled to Dunton after robbing a bank at Telluride.

Nearly half of Dunton's residents worked at the Emma. When the mines began to dwindle after the turn of the century, so did the population. The pastoral splendor of the isolated community was not enough to hold those who were miners by trade.

Buildings have been re-roofed and well-preserved. Today Dunton attracts fishermen, hunters, hikers, and cross-country skiers.

● ●

Wagons stop opposite Mary Brown's Bon Ton Restaurant at Rico, where meals cost thirty-five cents. *Denver Public Library, Western History Department.*

Rico, at the turn of the century. *Collection of Dave Southworth.*

SAN JUAN COUNTY

• •

SILVERTON

Location: 49 miles north of Durango on U.S. Highway 550

Prior to the Brunot Agreement of September 1873, the Ute Indians, led by Chief Ouray, roamed the mountains and valleys of the San Juans. Consequently very little prospecting took place during that time. Some which did, however, is worthy of note. In mid-October 1860, on his second journey into the San Juans, Charles Baker led a party of (150?) men into the Animas Valley. Most of the group camped at Baker's Park (the future site of Silverton). According to Baker, members of his party were rewarded with values of from three to twenty-five cents per pan. The tent colony which sprang up was called Baker's City.

The threat of Indians and the Civil War minimized activity in the area for many years, until Dempsey Reese and his partners began the first productive mining at the Little Giant in 1871. Once again Baker's Park was home to new settlers. There are conflicting reports as to who built the first cabin in the vicinity. Tom Blair could have constructed the first cabin (in what later became known as Arastra Gulch)—then again, it could have been Col. Francis M. Snowden—or possibly even John P. Johnson. Reese built his cabin north of town on Cement Creek. The Brunot Agreement, which opened the area for white settlers, was actually ratified in 1874—and the townsite of Silverton was surveyed that same year. The group which weathered in for their first winter that year included eight women. Pete Schneider delivered water in barrels to the earliest townspeople and became wealthy by selling it for fifty cents per bucket. The sheriff was also the mail carrier. Mrs. W. E. Earl led the campaign to raise funds for a schoolhouse. Upon its completion the structure also housed the first town offices and was used for church services as well. The first addition of John Curry's *La Plata Miner* rolled off the press on July 10, 1875.

Among the earliest businesses in Silverton (those established by 1875) were the general store of Greene & Company, R. C. Luesley's general merchandise store, the drugstore of B. A. Taft, the Ambold Brothers' Meat Market, and an assay office. Also, there were attorneys' offices, a doctor's office, a post office, but no jail house. The first lawbreaker was chained to the floor of a cabin. There were places to eat and drink, and there was the Briggs House—a log hotel constructed by J. L. Briggs (it was renamed the Silverton Hotel in 1876). Lodging was also available at the Centennial Hotel (later known as the Walker House). There were also two smelters and a sawmill. The late 1870s brought continued growth to Silverton. Construction throughout this period was all wood frame. The year 1880 marked the beginning of brick and stone construction, and many of the buildings which exist today were built during the ensuing period. The east-west streets in Silverton are numbered. Those running north and south have names. The main street through the central business district is Greene Street. Most of the saloons, gambling dens, and brothels were located one block to the east on Blair Street.

Prior to the arrival of the railroad it was difficult to haul gold and silver ores from the mines in the San Juans. Pack trains could negotiate the mountain passes only during the summer, at which time it was necessary to haul in supplies for those months when Silverton was inaccessible. During the fall of 1881 the Denver & Rio Grande began laying rails from Durango to Silverton. By early 1882, the town which awaited arrival of the railroad consisted of about 300 homes, two hotels, a schoolhouse and church, two sawmills, two brick works, a few buildings related to mining, and about 75 other business establishments. The arrival of the Denver & Rio Grande into Silverton on July 13, 1882, marked the beginning of the town's greatest period of growth.

Englishman W. S. Thomson began construction in 1882 on one of Silverton's finest buildings. The elegant Grand Hotel (later renamed the Hotel Imperial, and then again changed to the Grand Imperial Hotel) was located at the corner of 12th and Greene Streets, had hotel rooms on the third floor, town offices and council rooms on the second floor, and leased space for four separate stores on the first floor (they originally housed two clothing stores and two hardware stores).

Blair Street was one of Colorado's most notorious red-light districts. It was lined with saloons, dance halls, gambling dens, elegant bordellos and seedy cribs—and it operated "wide open" twenty-four hours a day. A popular bordello was Jack Gilheany's "Laundry." According to one source, "If you went in with any money, you came out clean." The Bon Ton, Diamond Belle, Monte Carlo, and the Tremount were some of the larger houses on Blair Street. Silverton continued to serve bootleg whiskey during Prohibition, without any pressure from local law enforcement officials. Everybody pitched in to move the whiskey to safe hiding whenever word was received that Federal Revenue agents were nearby.

Like many towns in the old west, Silverton had a few gunfights. In October 1878, after an argument and fistfight between Tom Milligan and Bill Connors, Connors advised Milligan that he would shoot him the next time he saw him. Shortly thereafter as Milligan was walking down Greene Street he spotted Connors in front of the Silverton Hotel. Both men drew and Milligan shot Connors through the stomach. He died three days later. Milligan was acquitted on the grounds of self defense.

There are several variations to the Harry Cleary story, and this is one of them. On August 23, 1879, Cleary and "Mexican Joe" became very rowdy while drinking at Brown and Cort's Saloon on Greene Street. James M. "Ten Die" Brown, one of the saloon's owners, escorted Cleary out the front door. Cleary turned and shot Brown. Brown was able to get off some shots, and one stray bullet hit handicapped night watchman Hiram Ward in the left shoulder. Ward, in turn, also shot Brown. Although it was more likely one of Ward's bullets that penetrated Brown's heart, Cleary was blamed for the killing, arrested and jailed. Late that night a mob dragged Cleary from the jail house and lynched him behind the blacksmith shop.

At 11 p.m. on August 24, 1881 La Plata County Sheriff, Luke Hunter, arrived in Silverton with warrants for the arrest of members of the Stockton-Eskridge gang. Burt Wilkinson, Dyson Eskridge, and Kid Thomas (a black man who was also known as the "Copper Colored Kid") had been drinking at the Diamond Saloon. Sheriff Hunter rounded up Silverton's marshal, D. C. (Clate) Ogsbury. As the two men walked down Greene Street, Wilkinson and Eskridge opened fire killing Ogsbury instantly. The two escaped on foot while Kid Thomas, who apparently fired no shots, rounded up their horses. He was apprehended near the stable and carried to jail. Once again, a mob took the law into its own hands as they dragged the black lad from jail and lynched him behind the old county building. Burt Wilkinson was turned in for a $2,500 reward by the gang leader Ike Stockton. Once again, the mob ruled. According to the *San Juan Herald*:

> " ... a party of masked men suddenly appeared before the guards at the jail and overpowered both of them and the jailer, went into the jail and seizing Wilkinson, passed the noose about his neck and asked him if he had anything to say before his death. He replied: 'Nothing, gentlemen, Adios!' He was perfectly composed to the very last, got up on a chair and assisted the vigilantes to hasten the hanging."

About a month later, Ike Stockton was shot in Durango by Deputy Sheriff Jim Sullivan. The bullet shattered Stockton's knee. Following amputation of his leg, Stockton bled to death.

There are many stories to tell about Silverton—and its many colorful residents. There were the earlier girls of Blair Street like Molly Foley and Blanche DeVille. Some of the prostitutes after the turn of the century had interesting names, such as "Diamond Tooth" Leona, "Jew" Fanny, "Nigger" Lola, and "Tar Baby" Brown. Ruthless town marshal Tom Cain was in the news consistently for his questionable activities. The famous Wyatt Earp ran the gaming rooms for a while at George Brower's fancy saloon and gambling hall, the Arlington. The famed Dodge City Cow Boy Band (the original spelling of cowboy was two words) of C. M. Beeson moved its headquarters to Silverton in June 1890, and operated from town for a few years until Buffalo Bill purchased the group which became part of his Wild West Show. Part of the Guggenheim fortune was reaped in the Silverton area. Multimillionaire Thomas Walsh of Camp Bird fame had mining interests in the region as well.

Mining was an important part of Silverton's economy. Some of the region's top mines were the Silver Lake, the Iowa and Tiger at Arastra Gulch, North Star, the famed Sunnyside (see Gladstone for discussion on the Sunnyside and American Tunnel), the Shenandoah, and the Dives. The latter two were later combined and operated by the Shenandoah-Dives Company, which also operated the North Star, the Terrible, and other properties. It also constructed a large mill in 1933.

The tourist industry is an important part of today's economy. The old coal-fired, steam-operated train runs daily during the season between Durango and Silverton. Since 1981 it has been operated by the Durango & Silverton Narrow Gauge Railroad Company (D&SNG) Additionally, there are many century-old buildings and other relics which reflect the old west that once was.

● ●

••

MINERAL POINT

Location: 8 miles southeast of Ouray

Prospectors Abe Burrows, who discovered the Burrows Mine, and Charles McIntyre founded the camp at Mineral Point in 1873. It was named for the large composite of quartz and other minerals located at the site. The rich vein of the Mastodan Mine extended through Mineral Point and on for several miles.

It is said the Old Lout Mine was thought to be worthless and in the process of being abandoned when one of the miners took one last shot and uncovered a rich body of ore. The mine yielded $86,000 the first month. There were other good mines in the area including the Red Cloud, the Vermillion, and the Bill Young. The San Juan Chief Mill was constructed above the city.

Mineral Point was located high in the mountains, below the crest of Engineer Pass, at an altitude of 11,474 feet. Winters were severe—even summer nights were cold. Its summer population was approximately 200. Stage service came from each side of the range. Silver ore was also shipped out in both directions for reduction—down to Lake City in the East and usually to Animas Forks on the western side. The camp had a hotel (which housed a saloon), a general store, several restaurants, and a saw mill.

The demonetization of silver caused by the repeal of the Sherman Silver Purchase Act in 1893, spelled doom for Mineral Point.

••

HOWARDSVILLE

Location: 4 miles northeast of Silverton

Howardsville was named for George W. Howard, who built the first permanent cabin in the community. By 1874 there were many homes, stores, and saloons, as well as a reduction works. At that time, the town was a part of La Plata County which included the area now covered by Ouray, San Juan, and parts of San Miguel and Dolores Counties. Howardsville became the first county seat selected in western Colorado. A few short months later, it was dumped as county seat. When La Plata County was divided, so were the records. The records for that portion which was to become San Juan County were moved to Silverton, the new county seat.

The area had good mines leading down from Stoney Pass, originally one of the main entrances into the San Juans, on to Howardsville at the head of Cunningham Gulch. The post office closed in 1939, but a few residents still live up in the Gulch.

••

• •

EUREKA

Location: 7 miles northeast of Silverton via State Highway 110 (east)

Alongside the Animas River, from the flat where the townsite of Eureka once existed, the foundations of the famed Sunnyside Mill (once one of the largest in Colorado) stair-step up the mountainside. The history of Eureka paralleled the history of the Sunnyside.

The Sunnyside Mine was located in 1873. At first it was a property of poor to average yield, and expensive to operate. Operating in the red, John Terry sold the property to a New York group for $300,000. After paying Terry a $75,000 down payment, they shortly became disenchanted with the mine and offered it back to Terry. With money in his pocket, Terry resumed operations. Before long the mine was producing very rich ore. The Sunnyside made Terry a millionaire. The property was worked continuously until it closed in 1931. It was renovated and reopened again—twice, closing again during World War II. The Sunnyside employed as many as five hundred persons during its most productive period. The American Tunnel (see Gladstone) was extended to tap the Sunnyside, and the mine continued to produce through most of the 1960s and '70s—in fact it has produced over six million tons of ore during its history. The Sunnyside Mine lease was purchased in 1985 by Canadian-owned Echo Bay Mines.

The area in and around Eureka had many mines and several mills. During the boom-days two thousand people lived in the community and most of them worked at the mining properties.

Otto Mears' Silverton-Northern Railroad arrived in Eureka in 1896. The railroad operated for many years, until the first closing of the Sunnyside.

At first Eureka only had one hotel, but after the turn of the century each of the large mills had its own boardinghouse. The business district was filled with the usual stores, saloons and restaurants. Eureka had a monthly newspaper —the *San Juan Expositor*—which was published by Theodore Comstock who later went on to found the School of Geology at the University of Arizona.

Eureka's history is marked by casualties and property damage from rock-slides and snowslides. Buildings at one edge of town and some of the mining properties were perilously close to the base of barren mountain slopes. The aforementioned foundations and a couple of structures are all that is left.

• •

● ●

ANIMAS FORKS

Location: 12 miles northeast of Silverton via State Highway 110

The town of Animas Forks was poorly platted in 1877, about two years after the first claims were staked. Those inhabitants who braved the harsh winters did so defensively, in the wake of snowstorms and dangerous drifts. As an enticement to live near timberline, settlers were offered free lots and construction assistance. Many responded, and the community blossomed.

The town was built with an air of permanence. Buildings were well-constructed with finished lumber and shingled roofs. False-fronted buildings lined the main street of town. By the mid-80s, Animas Forks had three hotels (the Mercer, Flagstaff, and Kalamazoo House), two assay offices, many stores and saloons, a telephone system, and a newspaper—the *Animas Forks Pioneer*. The jailhouse, which contained two cells, was constructed entirely of two-by-sixes laid flat. At the south edge of town stood the huge Gold Prince Mill.

The boardinghouse of Mrs. Eckard was very popular with miners in the Animas Forks' area—and so was she. Once a freeloader absconded without paying three months' board. A "posse" of Mrs. Eckard's friends found the scalawag in Silverton and offered him a choice—pay up or be hanged. Mrs. Eckard received her money, and no one ever cheated her again.

The Gold Prince was the most productive mine in the area. Other valuable mining properties included the Early Bird, Columbia, Silver Coin, Red Cloud, Eclipse, Little Arthur, and the Iron Cap.

Near the turn of the century, famed pathfinder Otto Mears built the Silverton Northern Railroad spur from Silverton, through Eureka, to Animas Forks.

Amidst the ruins of Animas Forks stands a once stately and elegant Victorian home. A prominent bay window faces toward the Animas River. Locals say it belonged to Thomas F. Walsh, discoverer of the famed Camp Bird Mine. One legend says, his daughter Evalyn Walsh McLean (once an owner of the Hope Diamond) was born here. Another indicates that she lived here while writing her biography, *Father Struck It Rich*. Evalyn was born in Denver and it is unlikely she ever lived in Animas Forks.

Although some mining continued, Animas Forks was a ghost town by 1923. The railroad bed once again became a road when the tracks were removed in 1942.

● ●

● ●

GLADSTONE

Location: 7 miles north of Silverton via State Highway 110 (west)

A chlorination works was constructed on the road up Cement Creek from Silverton to Poughkeepsie—a short-lived mining camp a few miles above. Gladstone began as a few employees established "residency" near the works.

The Sampson Mine was located in 1882. Other discoveries followed. The story of Gladstone, however, is centered around the Gold King Mine. In 1887, Olaf Nelson, discovered a good vein while working the Sampson. With the thought that there might be more rich ore nearby, he staked out an adjacent claim. Nelson worked his claim on a part time basis for three years until his death. His widow sold the Gold King in 1894 to Cyrus Davis and Henry Soule for the sum of $15,000. The new owners invested more into the property and the expansion paid off. The mine yielded over one million dollars during the next three years. Much of its success was due to Willis Kinney, who managed the mine and originally suggested its purchase.

The prosperity of Gladstone paralleled that of the Gold King. Rows of white company owned cottages sprang up to house employees. Gladstone, which was named for the Prime Minister of Great Britain, had boardinghouses, restaurants, saloons, and dance halls. There was a newspaper, the *Gladstone Kibosh*. A smelter was constructed. The arrival in 1899 of Otto Mears' Silverton, Gladstone and Northerly Railroad, a narrow gauge, was cause for much celebration.

Tragedy struck the Gold King Mine in 1907 when fire trapped three miners. Two of the three, and four rescuers, died as a result of smoke inhalation. Further trouble beset the mine when litigation between heirs and stockholders closed the property in 1910. The mine reopened in 1918, again under the management of Kinney.

The American Tunnel Project of Standard Metals was started in 1959 when construction began to enlarge and extend the Gold King Tunnel (already one mile long) in order to tap the lower extensions of the Sunnyside Mine (also see Eureka). An average of 600 tons of ore were processed per day through the 1960s. Since then production has been on an off again-on again basis. On Sunday, June 4, 1978 disaster struck. The spur vein of the Sunnyside was being mined seventy feet below Lake Emma which broke through dumping thousands of gallons of water and a million tons of mud into the mine—a mess which required two years to clean up. Luckily nobody was killed as the entire crew of 125 workers had the day off when the breakthrough occurred. The project closed in 1991.

● ●

Burros on Silverton's 13th Street are loaded with track rails for the mines. *Denver Public Library, Western History Department.*

This county jail at Silverton was completed in 1902. It now houses the San Juan County Historical Society Museum. *Dave Southworth.*

The United Church of Christ at Silverton was established in 1876. *Nancy Flanders.*

A deserted building at Howardsville. *Dave Southworth.*

A stroll down the main street of Eureka. The most distant false-front on the right side was the general merchandise and meat store of A. W. Helmboldt, which operated between 1893 and 1902. *Colorado Historical Society.*

The Sunnyside Mill stair-steps up the mountainside at Eureka.
Colorado Historical Society.

Animas Forks is an interesting ghost town
in a picturesque setting. *Dave Southworth.*

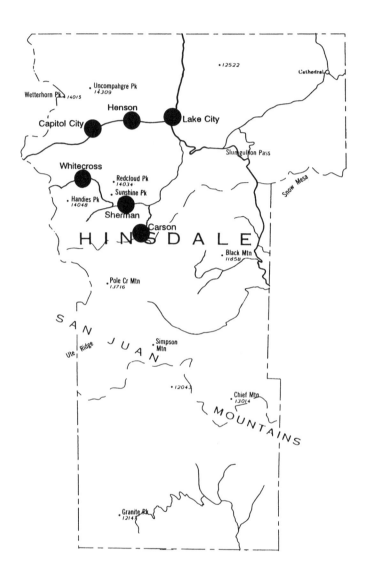

HINSDALE COUNTY

• •

LAKE CITY

Location: 55 miles south of Gunnison on State Highway 149

The Ute Indians occupied the area which was to become Lake City until the Brunot Agreement (which was ratified in 1874) opened the area for white settlers. The Ute-Ulay Mine, located in 1871 (see Henson), was the first gold strike in the area. The mine, located west of town, could not be developed until after the relocation of the Indians. The Golden Fleece (originally named the Hotchkiss Mine for its discoverer Enos Hotchkiss) was discovered in 1874. The mine, which had many ownership changes, was the best producer in the area. The Belle of the West and other strikes followed. The development of Lake City was well on its way.

By 1876 the community had four hotels, seven saloons, a newspaper, the *Silver World*, and the first church on the western slope—the Presbyterian Church. A reduction plant, which was powered by a seventy foot waterfall, was constructed above the community at Granite Falls.

Lake City had a wild red-light district. In Hell's Acre, as it was called, gambling dens and dance halls were mixed with the many brothels and the Crystal Palace—the posh bordello of Clara Ogden. One of the joints was owned by two characters named Betts and Browning, who had a propensity for thievery. In 1882, during a confrontation with the law, the pair shot and killed Sheriff E. N. Campbell. Betts and Browning fled but were captured by a posse and jailed. The community was irate. A raging lynch-mob dragged the pair out of jail and hung them from a nearby bridge.

Lake City had a legendary preacher, Rev. George M. Darley, who documented his tribulations. He preached the gospel in the most unlikely places. Darley believed that the folks who needed religion the most were the ones who lived in, and frequented, Hell's Acre, so he spread the holy word in gambling dens and dance halls.

Another church was built. Two more newspapers began publishing, the *Mining Register* and the *Lake City Phonograph*. Two banks and a library were constructed, and the stone schoolhouse was built in 1882. People came from great distances to shop at Lake City's large variety of stores. The city also had one of the earliest telephone systems in the state.

After the Denver & Rio Grande arrived in 1889, mines near some of the high mountain camps such as Whitecross, Sherman, and Carson shipped their ores by wagon as far as twenty five miles to reach the railroad at Lake City.

Lake City, which had a population of about 4,000 at its peak, was a socially active community. Dances, concerts, and banquets were commonplace. There were several clubs, civic organizations, and many other group functions. Much of the social activity centered around the churches and the Occidental Hotel.

In 1874 at the foot of Slumgullion Pass, the remains of five men were discovered. One had been shot, the other four had their skulls crushed. Each of the bodies had been carved up and fleshy parts removed. Herein lies the legend of Alferd Packer—that part of history for which Lake City is most famous.

Packer and five men were prospecting in the San Juan Mountains during the winter of '73-74. During the spring, Packer arrived alone at the Los Pinos Indian Agency near Saguache, stating that the others had left him and that he nearly starved on his trek back to civilization. After the bodies were found, Packer was arrested and charged with cannibalism. He escaped but was arrested again nine years later in Wyoming and returned to Lake City for trial. He received the death sentence. He won a new trial in Gunnison and received a prison term, which several years later was followed by a pardon. *Denver Post* newswoman, Polly Pry, who had crusaded for his release, was instrumental in getting Packer a job as doorman at the Post.

No other incidents of cannibalism have ever been tried in the United States court system. When sentence was first pronounced, according to legend and poet Stella Pavich, the judge told Packer: "...There was siven Dimmycrats in Hinsdale County! But you, yah voracious, man-eatin son of a b____, Yah et five of them, therefore I sentence ye T' be hanged by the neck ontil y're dead, dead, dead!" The comical and often-repeated quotation was not a statement from Judge M.B. Gerry, an articulate gentleman.

A commemorative to the men lies at the foot of Slumgullion Pass. Isn't it strange that the site where Alferd Packer allegedly had his meals is named after a miner's stew—slumgullion?

One of Lake City's most famous visitors was Susan B. Anthony. In 1877 a huge crowd gathered around the courthouse steps to hear her lecture on women's suffrage.

Lake City, which was named for Lake San Cristobal, never became a ghost town—probably because of its many stone structures. The population dwindled to a couple of hundred people. The railroad tracks were removed in 1937; the Golden Fleece Mine was sold for taxes in 1943; the Occidental Hotel burned down in 1944; but Lake City has emerged as the peaceful and lovely community that it is today.

• •

HENSON

Location: 7 miles west of Lake City on the road to Engineer Pass

Henry Henson, for whom the town is named, and his partners Joel K. Mullen, Albert Mead, and Charles Goodwin struck gold in 1871 and located the Ute-Ulay Mine. The discovery, which was on Indian land, brought more prospectors into the area much to the outcry of the Ute Indians. The white settlers temporarily vacated the area. In 1874 the Brunot Agreement was ratified, which opened the San Juan Mountains for settlement. Henson and his partners returned to their claims, were successful, and in 1876 sold to Crooke Bros. of Lake City for

$125,000. Crooke Bros. added a lead smelter which operated on ore from the area mines. In 1880 the property sold again for $1,200,000. In 1882 a concentrator was erected. By 1893 the plant was the largest in the San Juans.

The town which grew up around the mines was very congested because the gulch was narrow, leaving little room for the many stores and houses that were constructed. In 1877 the Henson Creek Road was extended to the west, topping the mountain range near Engineer Peak, and connecting with the Animas Forks Road to Ouray and Silverton.

Henson was a tough town. During its short history, labor problems, accidents, and shootings were commonplace. Through a miscalculation in tunneling, shafts from the Ute-Ulay and Hidden Treasure mines made connection. An explosion of gas released in the tunnels resulted in thirty-six casualties. Eighty Italian members of the Western Federation of Miners Union struck at the Ute-Ulay and Hidden Treasure Mines in 1899. They were tough, armed, and physically drove off all others attempting to work. The Italian Consul and the militia were called in to coax the union workers into surrendering. This was accomplished. Three days after their arrest, the company made an announcement advising that they would employ no more Italians. All single Italian miners were ordered to leave the county within three days and all married men within sixty days. The Italians left peacefully. The community declined, however, and the post office was discontinued fourteen years later.

••

CAPITOL CITY

Location: 10 miles west of Lake City on the road to Engineer Pass

Several good silver strikes in 1877 brought throngs of prospectors into the area. A townsite was platted, and tents were quickly replaced by substantial structures. George S. Lee built a sawmill to aid in the construction of Capitol City. Saloons, hotels, restaurants, and a general merchandise store sprang up. A post office was established in May of 1877.

Lee also constructed a smelter in 1879 along Henson Creek to process ore from the many mines nearby. The Ocean Wave Mine, which was located near the smelter, was one of the better producers in the vicinity. Other top mines were the Morning Star, Capitol City, Yellow Medicine, and Polar Star. Much litigation over claim rights hampered the total production of the area.

George S. Lee built a large and elegant brick home. In the house, which even contained a ballroom and orchestra pit, he and Mrs. Lee lavishly entertained guests from near and far. It is said that Lee had a dream that his town would become the capitol of Colorado (hence the name Capitol City) and that his home would become the governor's mansion. History has shown that Mr. Lee was overly optimistic with regard to the growth of the community.

After telephone service was established, a unique musical recital was held in 1881. Residents of Capitol City, Lake City, and communities as far as Silverton, who had telephones could pick up their receiver at a specified time and listen to the concert. In those days party lines could be connected.

The devaluation of silver in 1893 had a crippling effect. A few residents remained, but most moved on. The community experienced a short revival when gold was discovered after the turn of the century. The post office was discontinued in October 1920.

On the road above Capitol City, at an altitude of 11,200 feet, is Rose's Cabin. Shortly after the Brunot Agreement (see Henson) opened up the area, Corydon Rose built a boardinghouse which housed a tavern and a restaurant as a stop for travelers on the road to Engineer Pass. Today, the remnant stands amidst a field of dandelions.

• •

SHERMAN

Location: 16 miles southwest of Lake City via State Highway 149 and the road to Cinnamon Pass (which follows the Lake Fork of the Gunnison River)

The site where the busy little mining camp of Sherman once existed is located in one of the most picturesque areas of Colorado. It is located in a lush wooded valley below Sunshine Peak—a fourteener. The scenic trail from Lake City to Animas Forks was originally a toll road. To or from Animas Forks required a fare of $2.00, while Lake City in the other direction was $2.50 either way.

Sherman began in 1877 because of successful placer and lode mining in the vicinity. The Black Wonder was the best mine, and produced well past the turn of the century. Other mines were the George Washington, Monster, Mountain View, Minnie Lee, Smile of Fortune, Clinton, and New Hope. The area yielded gold, silver, copper, and lead. Most of the ores were transported to the smelters at Lake City for reduction.

The townsite, which was platted with wide streets, was dominated by three buildings. There was the camp's only hotel—the Sherman House. A mini-mall of sorts housed a general merchandise store, grocery, butcher shop, bakery, and even a bunkhouse. The Black Wonder Mill was located in town as well. Sherman was a convenient stagecoach stop, for its location is nearly midway between Lake City and Animas Forks. Population of the community peaked at about 300.

Snare Creek, Cataract Creek, and other tributaries dumped into Cottonwood Creek which intersects with the Lake Fork of the Gunnison River at Sherman. The valley was continually troubled with floods as a result of the heavy spring runoff. In an effort to control the water, a large dam was constructed. Shortly after it was completed, torrential rains flooded the gulches—tore through the dam, and destroyed much of the townsite.

• •

• •

WHITECROSS

*Location: 21 miles southwest of Lake City via State Highway 149 and the road
to Cinnamon Pass (along the Lake Fork of the Gunnison River)*

Two veins of white quartz cross each other high on the face of Whitecross
Mountain—hence the name of the mountain and the mining camp. A cluster of
mining camps blossomed in the spectacular high alpine meadow of Burrows
Park. Whitecross was the largest, and center of activity for the group which also
included the camps of Tellurium, Sterling, Burrows Park, and Argentum. They all
sprang to life between 1877 and 1880 following rich silver strikes in the vicinity.
The post office was established in 1880 as Burrows Park (but was actually located
at Whitecross). The name of the post office was changed to Whitecross in 1882.
The community maintained a summer population of about 200. The Hotel de
Clauson at Whitecross was the favorite meeting place for all of the neighboring
camps.

The Tabasco, Champion, Cracker Jack, and Bonhomme were the top mines.
The huge Tabasco Mill was constructed in 1901 just west of town. Burrows Park
(the camp) had three good producers—the Undine, Napoleon, and the Oneida
mines. The economy of Tellurium and Sterling relied on the Providence, Troy,
Mountain King, Allen Dale and the Little Sarah. The latter group of mines either
pinched-out early or were underdeveloped, and the short-lived camps of Tellurium
and Sterling became abandoned. The railroad was just a few miles away at
Animas Forks, but the road was so difficult that most ores were shipped to Lake
City for reduction. Repeal of the Sherman Silver Purchase Act spelled doom for
the silver industry and the remaining camps in Burrows Park became ghost
towns.

• •

CARSON

Location: Atop the Continental Divide, 11 miles south of Lake City

Carson straddles the top of the Continental Divide with parts of the camp
on each side. Actually there are two sites—one higher and older which was a
silver camp, the other lower and newer which was a gold camp. Situated at an
altitude of nearly 12,000 feet, and covered with snow most of the year, Carson
was often totally inaccessible.

Christopher J. Carson found traces of gold and silver in 1881 and staked
his claim—the Bonanza King. Carson Camp (as it was first named) was
established the following year.

Mines peppered the mountainsides. The St. Jacob's Mine was the area's
top producer. Its yield in 1898 alone was $190,000. Other productive mines were

the Thor, Maid of Carson, Legal Tender, Chandler, Kit Carson, and the Iron Mask, to name a few. Construction of the wagon road up Lost Trail Creek in 1887 facilitated shipment of ore out of, and supplies into, the area.

There are different theories as to the existence of two Carsons. Robert L. Brown's assessment seems most logical. Basically, he contends that the older Carson was predominantly a silver producing community—which it was. It probably faded after the silver panic of 1893. With new gold discoveries in 1896, the newer site sprang up near the Bachelor Mine, a gold producer. As the sites are close together, and whereas one was possibly abandoned when the other began, it is logical that they had the same name.

While the elements are taking their toll on the original Carson, the lower townsite is nicely withstanding the test of time.

● ●

The Hough Fire Company at Lake City in 1905. *Colorado Historical Society.*

The Presbyterian Church at Lake City was the first church built on the Western Slope. *Denver Public Library, Western History Department.*

Shops on Silver Street at Lake City. *Dave Southworth.*

The ruptured dam at Henson. *Dave Southworth.*

Capitol City today. *Dave Southworth.*

A wintery look at early Sherman. *Collection of Dave Southworth.*

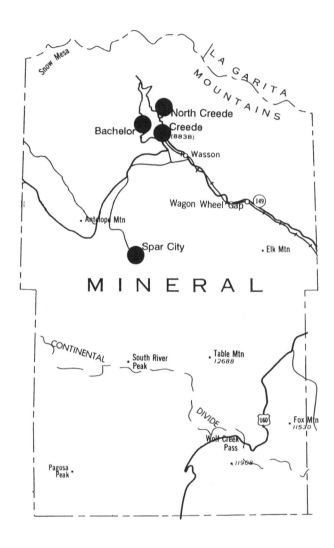

MINERAL COUNTY

• •

BACHELOR

Location: Near Creede, on the Bachelor Loop, via the south loop (Road #504) west and then north from Creede for a distance of four miles.

In September of 1891, Mr. and Mrs. C. L. Calvin constructed a home and a boardinghouse, which were the first buildings erected in the town of Bachelor. Shortly thereafter, the Last Chance Mine struck paydirt, which coupled with other mining activity in the winter of 1891-92 created a bustling and rowdy boom town. Fortune seekers flocked to Bachelor Mountain by the hundreds, digging everywhere including the site of the planned city of Bachelor. After the chaos subsided another happening contributed to the population boom. Many citizens from nearby Creede moved to the high mountain town site after the disastrous fire in Creede on June 5, 1892. There seems to be no accurate source for Bachelor's peak population. Estimates range from 1,200 to as high as 6,000 during the boom period.

Following the Calvin's boardinghouse, the first three "businesses" to spring up were two saloons and a parlor house—a reflection of the wild nature of the community. Shootings, accidents, and fires were common occurrences. An excellent fire fighting brigade checked and controlled the fires, however, so the town avoided the type of devastation suffered by Creede.

A sad story is told about the town's reforming minister. One winter when his small daughter was dangerously ill with pneumonia, the minister traveled down to Creede to fetch a doctor. Upon returning home, he found a strange man hovering over his daughter's bed. Thinking the man was up to no good, he killed him on the spot. After learning the man was a doctor attempting to help his daughter, the minister was distraught and committed suicide. His daughter also died of her illness. A gravesite located below Bachelor in a grove of aspen is said to contain the bodies of the minister, his daughter and the doctor. Supposedly they are buried one on top of the other because of the difficulty of digging graves in the frozen ground of winter.

Like other mining communities there were parlor houses, gambling halls, and saloons. There must have been a little culture in Bachelor, however, for it had its own opera house, and the Bachelor City Dramatic Club which was touted as being excellent. The town also had its churches. The Congregational Church boasted that it was the highest church in the United States (the elevation of the town was 10,526).

The mines in the Bachelor area were among the richest in the Creede district. The boom and the glory were short lived, however. The silver devaluation in 1893 dealt Bachelor a severe blow. Although the town held on for several years, most of the residents moved off the mountain, down to Creede or elsewhere. Today, one partially roofed cabin, surrounded by trees, and the remains of two other cabins are all that exist at the site of Bachelor.

• •

••

NORTH CREEDE

Location: 1 mile north of Creede

The area "between the cliffs" was the first hub of activity in the vicinity. It was originally known as Creede, then Upper Creede when Jimtown to the south became Creede. Eventually it was renamed North Creede.

The community, set in a narrow and deep gorge, was and is a dangerous place to live. Heavy rains and melting snow cause the water level to run high. Each year threatening torrents of water roar through the area. A flood in 1918 washed away the Cliff Hotel and the Holy Moses Saloon as well as the section known as Stringtown. North Creede was devastated. Nevertheless, several buildings which hug the cliff wall have resisted floods, fire and the test of time.

During its boom years, North Creede had a population of several hundred. Today there is only a handful of residents in this picturesque suburb of Creede.

••

CREEDE

Although a little prior prospecting was done in the vicinity, nothing spectacular happened until 1889. Nicholas C. Creede and his partner George L. Smith discovered float near the junction of West Willow and East Willow Creeks. They traced the source to the head of West Willow Creek, made a claim, and named it the Holy Moses. The men left prior to the ensuing cold winter, and returned in the spring of 1890. David H. Moffat, president of the Denver and Rio Grande Railroad, and a group of others, purchased the claim almost immediately, for $70,000. This triggered one of the great booms in Colorado history.

In 1891 Theodore Renniger, grubstaked by his former boss Ralph Granger, discovered what the assayer called the richest stuff he had ever seen. They staked their claim which they called the Last Chance. Nearby, Nicholas Creede located the Amethyst Mine. These two mines were the richest silver producing mines in the Creede district during the 1890s.

Several camps cropped up between the cliffs, up the canyon, and spread to the small valley south of the cliffs. Originally, the area of the canyon by the junction of West Willow Creek and East Willow Creek was considered Creede. The area south of the fork was called Stringtown because it was so narrow between the cliffs. As the population spread south beyond the cliffs, Jimtown was established as the commercial center of the area. Jimtown was the approximate location of Creede today. The area north of the forks, originally known as Creede, became Upper Creede, and later officially North Creede. Additionally, Weaver blossomed beyond North Creede on West Willow Creek; Bachelor was established high on the mountain above Jimtown; and Sunnyside sprang into existence over the hill to the west of Bachelor.

Speculators, miners, gamblers, and parlor girls came on every train to the overcrowded vicinity. The population swelled to about 10,000. If ever there was a red-hot town, Creede was it. It was a melting pot of strange, different, and interesting people. Soapy Smith, a slick and intelligent con-artist, and his gang ruled the city for a while. Smith opened the Orleans Club and declared himself boss of the underworld. Bob Ford (the name who killed Jesse James) built a dance hall and saloon called the Exchange. On June 8, 1892, Ford was slain by a shotgun blast from Ed O'Kelley. O'Kelley was convicted, imprisoned and then pardoned a few years later. Ford's body was buried on Boot Hill, and remained there for a few years before his family transported it back to Missouri. Shortly after the body was removed, another killer was buried in the same grave. Another saloon, which was owned by a Denver firm, was managed by Bat Masterson.

The parlor houses were operated by Lulu Slain, her friend the Mormon Queen, Slanting Annie, Lillie Lovell, and Rose Vastine, known as "Timberline" for obvious reasons—she was six feet two inches tall. These "beauties" prompted the *Creede Candle* of April 29, 1892, to write: "Creede is unfortunate in getting more of the flotsam of the state than usually falls to the lot of mining camps —some of her citizens would take sweepstake prizes at a hog show."

At one time or another Creede also had three cigar-smoking women gamblers —Poker Alice, Calamity Jane, and Killarney Kate.

The history of Creede follows the boom and bust pattern of many mining communities. In 1892 a fire started in a saloon, spread down Creede Avenue, and eventually destroyed most of the business district. The fire and the silver crash of 1893 created a mass exodus and spelled the end of the boom.

Creede today is a friendly town—proud of its rich mining heritage, and ready to share it with the many tourists who visit each year.

• •

SPAR CITY

Location: 14 miles southwest of Creede via State Highway 149 and Lime Creek Road

The picturesque camp was established in the spring of 1892 as Fisher City, after an early discoverer of float gold. It was also known as Lime Creek before being renamed for the Big Spar Mine.

By the summer of 1892 there were about 300 residents in the community, with many more in the surrounding hills. A saw mill was constructed. Main Street sprang up with the usual saloons, restaurants, and stores. *The Creede Candle* opened a newspaper office to publish *The Spar City Spark*.

A stage line was established between Spar City and Creede as well. The road to Creede ran over Robber's Hill, so named because it was a favorite ambush point for highwaymen.

A claim to fame for Spar City was a big pine bar which graced the principal saloon. Bob Ford, the man who gunned down Jesse James, was shot to death in his Exchange Club at Creede behind his own bar. A saloon keeper in Spar City, wanting the memento, purchased the bar and had it shipped by wagon with great difficulty to his establishment.

Spar City today consists of well-kept cabins, many of which still form a neat row down each side of Main Street. The community is private, fenced, and has a "No Trespassing—Members Only" sign at the gate. Special permission should be obtained before entering the premises.

• •

Townspeople line up for a photograph at Bachelor. *Colorado Historical Society.*

A house at Bachelor is hidden by trees. *Dave Southworth.*

All the comforts of home and "no danger of fire" at this Creede hotel.
Colorado Historical Society.

Creede Avenue was a busy place. *Colorado Historical Society.*

This Creede building was once an assay office. *DaveSouthworth.*

The main street of Spar City was called North Street. *DaveSouthworth.*

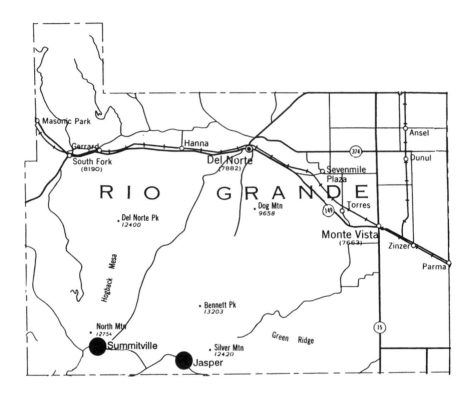

RIO GRANDE COUNTY

• •

SUMMITVILLE

Location: 24 miles southwest of Del Norte

John Esmund discovered gold high on South Mountain in 1870. Each summer he worked the site, extracting an abundance of rich ore. He returned in the spring of 1873 to find that his claim had been jumped. Others were working his mine. Esmund had failed to do the necessary paperwork to properly establish his claim. The Little Annie became the best producer in the area. Although he was discouraged, Esmund knew there was much more gold in the area. He moved around the slope and made two new strikes—the Major and the Esmund (later called the Aztec). Having learned a valuable lesson, he did the proper paperwork on these claims.

Two brothers, James and William Wightman (for whom Wightman Creek is named), also discovered gold on South Mountain in 1870. Other strikes followed, and Summitville became a bustling gold camp.

By 1882 Summitville had a population of over 1,000, several hotels, a newspaper *The Summitville Nugget*, many stores and saloons, and nine mills to process ore from the mines.

The nearby city of Del Norte was important to the history of Summitville. Del Norte was an important shipping point, stagecoach junction, and supply center. It also had a resident who was instrumental in the success of Summitville. The suave and colorful Tom Bowen struck it rich with his Little Ida Mine. Bowen wore many hats. At one time or another he was a lawyer, Governor of the Idaho Territory, brigadier general in the Union army, district judge, Senator, and heavy gambler. The Little Ida was the catalyst which created a fortune for Tom Bowen. He purchased many other mining properties, including the Little Annie.

In 1885 several of the mines including the Little Annie ran into financial difficulties. The population of Summitville rapidly declined. By 1892 the town had only a handful of inhabitants. Mining in the vicinity experienced a few revivals. One occurred just before the turn of the century and another in the 1930s. The greatest production, however, has been in recent years. The heavy trucks and equipment of Galactic Resources, Ltd. have been rolling back and forth through the uninhabited and slowly deteriorating ghost town of Summitville. Galactic suffered heavy losses through 1991, sold the balance of its mining interests, and in late 1992 considered a reclamation project as a way to bounce back. The January 28, 1993 *Wall Street Journal* advised that Galactic Resources, Ltd. had filed for bankruptcy. Many buildings still exist at the high-mountain site of Summitville—one of Colorado's more interesting ghost towns.

• •

● ●

JASPER

Location: 22 miles east of Summitville on Forest Route 250

In 1880 several strikes were made in the mountains around the Alamosa River. John Cornwall and a group of founding fathers established a settlement in the high mountain valley along the river.

The community was originally named Cornwall—then changed to Jasper. Nearby, Cornwall Mountain retained its name. When the post office was established in November 1882, Cornwall was named postmaster. One of the earliest settlers, Alva Adams, later became Governor of Colorado.

A fair amount of mining was done at the Sanger Mine, the Perry Mine, and others. In 1887 ten tons of ore were shipped to a smelter in Denver for refinement. Jasper miners never knew the result of the analysis because the smelter burned to the ground with the ore inside.

There must have been many teetotalers amongst the miners in the area. Jasper's only saloon went out of business long before the town began to fade.

● ●

Following gold strikes on South Mountain, Summitville became a bustling mining town. *Denver Public Library, Western History Department.*

There are many creaking structures throughout Summitville. *Dave Southworth.*

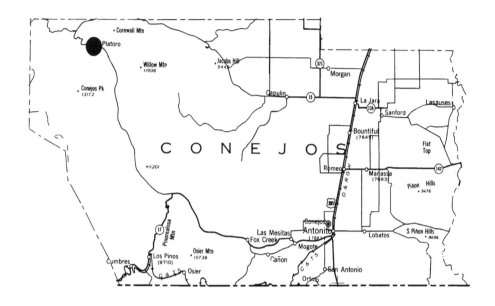

CONEJOS COUNTY

• •

PLATORO

Location: 20 miles south of Summitville via Forest Route 330 and 380

Platoro sprang to life in 1882 when rich ore was discovered in the area. The town was platted in a flat, high mountain valley (altitude: 9,700 ft.) near the most northerly bend of the Conejos River.

Two mountains south of town bear the names of two of the earliest mine discoveries, the Mammoth and Forest King. Other good mines were the Anchor, Puzzler, Last Chance, Parole, and the Pass-Me-By.

Platoro was one of the highest mining towns in the region. It had a tough existence for several years. Ores had to be packed out by burro and supplies brought in the same way. A wagon road from Summitville was completed in 1888, and Platoro became more accessible. A post office was established in March of the same year. The community had a population of about 300 in 1890.

Ores taken from the area were never more than average in quality. As production declined many miners packed up and left. Platoro experienced a couple of upturns after the turn of the century but neither developed into much.

The town which was named for "plata" and "oro", Spanish for silver and gold, is very much intact today. Cabins have been renovated and many are summer tourist rentals.

• •

Otto Blake's large cabin is at left. The canvas structure beyond it is the Platoro Hotel. The general store flies an American flag, at right. *Denver Public Library, Western History Department.*

Unlike this building, most of Platoro is inhabited. *Dave Southworth.*

Glossary of Mining Terms

ALLUVIAL DEPOSIT: Sediment deposited by a stream.

ARASTRA: An old Spanish apparatus used to break up ore by means of a heavy stone dragged around a circular trough.

ASSAY: To test and examine ores and minerals by a chemical process or the blowpipe method. Sometimes the assaying process requires the separation of precious metals from base metals by use of a cupel.

BAR: The peripheral accumulation of rocks along the banks of a stream, often worked for gold by prospectors.

CARBONATES: Those ores containing a large amount of carbonate of lead.

CLAIM: A mining claim is the right, or claim, of an individual or company to a specific location with set boundaries, and recorded according to law. Mining laws consider a claim legitimate if sufficient quantities of a metallic or other substance are found rendering the land valuable. Deposits of certain minerals, such as coal and oil, are the property of the United States and are not subject to claim under United States mining laws.

CONCENTRATION: The process by which nonessential and less valuable portions of ore are removed by mechanical means.

CRADLE: See Rocker.

CRIBBING: The process of constructing close timber, such as bulkheading or lining of a shaft.

CROSSCUT TUNNEL: A transverse tunnel which intersects a main tunnel, or drift, at an angle and leads to another point.

CUPEL: A small porous cup used in the assaying process of separate precious metals from lead and other base metals.

DREDGE: Bucket dredges and traction dredges are operated by power and usually are mounted on a boat. The bucket operates like an elevator and brings continuous loads of sand and gravel to the deck where it passes through a sluice. Traction dredges scoop much in the manner of a steam shovel. Suction dredges are smaller and often portable.

DRIFT: An underground tunnel which follows a vein. Usually the mine's main tunnel.

FISSURE VEIN: A crack in the earth's surface rock which is filled with a mineral matter other than that of its surrounding walls.

FLOAT: Pieces of ore which have washed away or have fallen from their parent veins. The discovery of float was usually the catalyst to trace each fragment toward its source.

GELENA: A common lead sulphide which often has silver content.

HYDRAULIC MINING: High pressure water is carried through a hose and nozzle and used to wash away gold bearing earth. The water and earth are carried through sluices which separate the gold.

IRON PYRITE: A mineral which resembles gold. Commonly called "fool's gold".

LODE: A vein or tabular deposit of precious mineral.

LONG TOM: A device used in the early mining days to aid in the separation of materials. Gravel is shoveled into the long tom, through which water is funneled, and worked with a hoe or rake. Gold and other heavier minerals are then swept through a screen and caught in the riffles beyond.

MILL: An establishment in which ores are reduced by means other than smelting.

MINE: Technically it is an ore deposit -- a rich or abundant source. Commonly considered the pit, excavation, or tunnel from which ores and precious minerals, etc. are taken from the earth.

MINING DISTRICT: An area of country usually located within certain natural boundaries, and designated by name, in which a substantial amount of mining activity occurs.

MOTHER LODE: The predominant vein, or lode, passing through a particular area. Prospectors dreamed of discovering a mother lode.

NUGGET: A lump of native precious metal (i.e. a gold nugget).

ORE DEPOSIT: The primary source of the mineral which occurs in a vein.

PAN: The slowest method in searching for gold is panning. Water is swirled in a circular motion over the earth and gravel in a flat shallow pan. Sand and earth are gradually washed away.

PLACER MINING: Surface deposit mining, as placer mining is sometimes called, is one of the oldest methods. Water action has already extracted the precious material and deposited it in more accessible places to be worked, such as stream beds, etc.

QUARTZ: A common opaque mineral sometimes found near richer deposits.

REDUCTION WORKS: Any plant which reduces metal from its ore (i.e. a smelting works).

RIFFLE: The bottom of a sluice or trough with slats spaced closely together in order to catch gold and other heavy minerals.

ROCKER: An early mining device is the rocker, sometimes called a cradle. Earth and gravel are shoveled into a sieve box in the top of the rocker. Water is channelled over the sieve as the device is rocked to and fro. Heavier gold filters to a trough where it is caught by the riffles.

SAMPLING WORKS: An establishment in which ores are sampled to determine their value.

SLUICE: In areas where there was a good water supply, the sluice was one of the most popular devices used by miners. Dirt is shoveled into the long trough with transverse riffles. The water flow washes away waste material leaving gold and other heavy materials in the riffles.

SMELTING: A process by which metals are reduced from their ores by fusion, in a furnace or crucible.

STAMP MILL: An establishment or works where rock is crushed by steam-powered or water-powered pestles or stamps (i.e. a quartz mill).

TAILINGS: Residue which is left behind after precious metals have been separated from the ore by concentration or dressing.

TELLURIDE: A rich ore containing compounds of tellurium and gold and/or silver.

TRAMWAY: A cable system, suspended between two points, by which ore or other material may be transported by buckets.

VEIN: An elongated mineral deposit, or fissure, often rich in content.

VUG: An open cavity in a rock or formation which is sometimes lined with crystalline deposits.

WILFLEY TABLE: A table used in ore dressing for concentrating and seperating various metals. A jerking motion allows light grains to wash over a riffled surface while heavy grains remain. An important Colorado invention which increased recovery and profits.

WIRE GOLD OR SILVER: Native gold or silver in a maze of wire-like threads.

Acknowledgements

My sincere appreciation to the following:

Nancy Flanders
Ruth S. Bennett
Teresa Bond
Hal Flanders
Ray B. Walling
Constant W. Southworth
Sue Anderson
Herb and Sheri Gable
Gene and Faye Franklin
Hayes Colburn
Kathey Swan, Bruce Hanson, Phil Panum, Kay Wisnia, Mary Daze, Britt Kaur
    and other staff members, Denver Public Library, Western History
    Department
Becky Lintz, Barbara Foley, David Halaas and David Wetzel, Colorado
    Historical Society, Stephen H. Hart Library
The Colorado History Museum
Cassandra M. Volpe, David M. Hays, Marilyn Burns, Marty Covey and Bruce
    Montgomery, University of Colorado at Boulder, Norlin Library
Robert E. Richardson, National Archives and Records Administration
Creed Historical Society
The National Mining Hall of Fame & Museum
Lake City Historical Museum
Lake City Chamber of Commerce
Museum of Western Colorado
Colorado School of Mines
Bureau of Mines
The Historical Museum of Silverton
Kris Maxfield, Silverton Chamber of Commerce
The Carnegie Library at Silverton
Allen Nossaman
The Animas Museum at Durango
The Colorado Outfitters Association
The U. S. Forest Service
Marilyn Peterson, Colorado Mountain Club
Beverly Rich, San Juan County Historical Society

Dave Southworth

Bibliography

BOOKS

Aldrich, John K. *My Favorite Ghosts*. Lakewood: Centennial Graphics, 1988.

Baker, James H., Editor. *History of Colorado*. Denver: Linderman Co., Inc., 1927.

Bateman, Alan M. *Economic Mineral Deposits*. New York: John Wiley and Sons, Inc., 1958.

Bates, Margaret. *A Quick History of Lake City, Colorado*. Colorado Springs: Little London Press, 1973.

Bauer, William H., James L. Ozment and John H. Willard. *Colorado Post Offices: 1859 -1989*. Golden: The Colorado Railroad Museum, 1990.

Benham, Jack L. *Camp Bird and the Revenue*. Ouray: Bear Creek Publishing Co., 1980.

Bird, Allan G. *Bordellos of Blair Street*. Grand Rapids: The Other Shop, 1987.

Bird, Allan G. *Silverton Gold*. Grand Rapids: The Other Shop, 1986.

Bird, Allan G. *Silverton: Then and Now*. Englewood: Access Publishing, 1990.

Brown, Robert L. *Colorado Ghost Towns-Past and Present*. Caldwell: Caxton Printers, 1977.

Brown, Robert L. *Jeep Trails to Colorado Ghost Towns*. Caldwell: Caxton Printers, 1978.

Bueler, Gladys R. *Colorado's Colorful Characters*. Boulder: Pruett Publishing Co., 1981.

Carter, William. *Ghost Towns of the West*. Menlo Park, CA: Lane Publishing Co., 1971.

Crofutt, George A. *Crofutt's Grip-Sack Guide of Colorado*. Boulder: Johnson Books, 1885.

Dallas, Sandra. *Colorado Ghost Towns and Mining Camps*. Norman: University of Oklahoma Press, 1985.

Dallas, Sandra. *Gaslights and Gingerbread*. Athens, OH: Swallow Press, 1965.

Dallas, Sandra. *No More than Five in a Bed: Colorado Hotels in the Old Days*. Norman: University of Oklahoma Press, 1967.

Dawson, John Frank. *Place Names In Colorado*. Denver: J. F. Dawson Publishing Co., 1954.

Dawson, Thomas F. and F.J.V. Skiff. *The Ute War*. Boulder: Johnson Publishing Co., 1980.

Decker, Sarah Platt (Durango Chapter D.A.R.). *Pioneers of the San Juan Country. Vol. I, II, III and IV.* Colorado Springs: The Out West Printing and Stationery Co., 1946 (1995 - new edition with indicies).

Eberhart, Perry. *Guide to the Colorado Ghost Towns and Mining Camps.* Denver: Sage Books, 1968.

Ellis, Amanda M. *Pioneers.* Colorado Springs: Dentan Publishing, 1955.

Ellis, Richard N. & Duane A. Smith. *Colorado: A History in Photographs.* Niwot: University Press of Colorado, 1991.

Fay, Abbott. *Famous Coloradans.* Ronia: Mountaintop Books, 1990.

Feitz, Leland. *Soapy Smith's Creede.* Colorado Springs: Little London Press, 1973.

Fetter, Richard L. and Suzanne Fetter. *Telluride: From Pick to Powder.* Caldwell: Caxton Printers, 1979.

Field, Eugene. *A Little Book of Western Verse.* New York: Charles Scribner's Sons, 1894.

Florin, Lambert. *Ghost Towns of the West.* New York: Promontory Press, 1970.

Fossett, Frank. *Colorado.* New York: C.G. Crawford, 1880.

George, R.D. *Colorado Geological Survey.* Denver: The Smith-Brooks Printing Co., 1909.

Grimstad, Bill. *The Last Gold Rush.* Victor: Pollux Press, 1983.

Hall, Frank. *History of the State of Colorado. 4 Vols.* Chicago: Blakely Printing Co., 1889, 1890, 1891, 1895.

Hollon, E. Eugene. *The Lost Pathfinder - Zebulon Montgomery Pike.* Norman: University of Oklahoma Press, 1949.

Hollister, Ovando J. *The Mines of Colorado.* Springfield, MA: Samuel Bowles & Company, 1867.

Hunt, Inez and Wanetta W. Draper. *To Colorado's Restless Ghosts.* Denver: Sage Books, 1960.

Jessen, Kenneth. *Eccentric Colorado.* Boulder: Pruett Publishing Company, 1985.

Jocknick, Sidney. *Early Days on the Western Slope of Colorado.* Glorieta, NM: Rio Grande Press, 1968.

Lamm, Richard D. and Duane A. Smith. *Pioneers and Politicians.* Boulder: Pruett Publishing Company, 1984.

McKenney's Business Directory of Principal Towns in California, Nevada, Utah, Wyoming, Colorado and Nebraska 1882. San Francisco: H.S. Crocker & Co., Publishers, 1882.

McLean, Evalyn Walsh. *Father Struck It Rich.* Boston: Little, Brown and Co., 1936.

Marshall, John B. and Temple H. Cornelius. *Golden Treasures of San Juan.* Athens: Swallow Press, 1990.

May, Stephen. *Pilgrimage: A Journey Through Colorado's History and Culture.* Athens, OH: Swallow Press, 1987.

Monnett, John H. *Colorado Profiles: Men and Women Who Shaped the Centennial State*. Evergreen: Cordillera Press, 1987.

Morris, John R. *Davis H. Waite: The Ideology of a Western Populist*. Washington, D.C.: University Press of America, 1982.

Noel, Thomas J. *Historical Atlas of Colorado*. Norman: University of Oklahoma Press, 1993.

Nossaman, Allen. *Many More Mountains. Volume 1: Silverton's Roots*. Sundance Books, 1989.

Olsen, Mary Ann. *The Silverton Story*. Cortez: Beaver Printing Co., 1962.

Pough, Frederick H. *A Field Guide to Rocks and Minerals*. Boston: Houghton Mifflin Company, 1955.

Prucha, Francis Paul. *American Indian Treaties: The History of a Political Anomaly*. Berkeley: University of California Press, 1994.

Rinehart, Frederick R. *Chronicles of Colorado*. Boulder: Roberts Rinehart, Inc., 1984.

Rockwell, Wilson. *Sunset Slope; True Epics of Western Colorado*. Denver: Big Mountain Press, 1956.

Schulze, Suzanne (Ed.). *A Century of the Colorado Census*. Greeley: University of Northern Colorado, 1976.

Smith, Duane A. *Rocky Mountain West*. Albuquerque: University of New Mexico Press, 1992.

Smith, P. David. *Ouray. Chief of the Utes*. Ouray: Wayfinder Press, 1986.

Ubbelohde, Carl. *A Colorado History*. Boulder: Pruett Press, Inc., 1965.

U.S. Bureau of the Census, Revised by the Social Science Research Council. *The Statistical History of the United States from Colonial Times to the Present*. Stanford: Fairfield Publishers, Inc., 1965.

Voynick, Stephen M. *The Making of a Hardrock Miner*. Berkeley: Howell-North, 1978.

Wolle, Muriel Sibell. *Stampede to Timberline*. Denver: Sage Books, 1962.

Wright, Carolyn and Clarence Wright. *Tiny Hinsdale of the Silvery San Juans*. Denver: Big Mountain Press, 1964.

NEWSPAPERS

Creede Candle

Denver Post

Denver Republican

Denver Times

Denver Tribune

Dolores News (Rico)

Durango Herald

Durango Record

Durango Democrat

Miner (Silverton)

Mineral County Miner (Creede)

Ouray Herald

Ouray Times

Republican (Telluride)

Rico Democrat

Rico Sun

Rio Grande Magazine

Rocky Mountain News

San Juan Herald

Silverton Democrat

Silverton Standard

Solid Muldoon (Ouray)

Telluride Journal

Wall Street Journal

ARTICLES

Colorado Historical Society. "Trails Through Time." *Colorado Heritage.* (Autumn 1990).

Halaas, David Fridtjof and Gerald C. Morton. "Boom and Bust: Images from the Colorado Chronicle." *Colorado Heritage.* Colorado Historical Society. (Issues 1 & 2, 1983).

James, Louise Boyd. "The Case of the Colorado Cannibal or `Have a Friend for Dinner'." *American West.* (February 1990).

Matthews, Carl F. "Rico, Colorado-Once a Roaring Camp." *Colorado Magazine* 28 (January 1951):37-49.

Naisbitt, John, Patricia Aburdene and John Vaughan. "West by Southwest: A Telluride Log House with Mining Camp Routes." *Architectural Digest* (June 1989):206(9).

Spence, Clark. "Western Mining." *Historians and the American West.* Michael Malone, editor. Lincoln: University of Nebraska Press, 1983.

Zavodni, Cathy. "Gold Mining Costs Keep Growing." *American Metal Market.* (June 17, 1991):A4.

OTHER SOURCES

American Metal Market - many brief articles too numerous to cite regarding the current Colorado mining scene and certain producers , with special recognition to authors Hassell Bradley and Christopher Munford.

Civil Works Administration, Thousand Town File, Unpublished, Colorado Historical Society, Denver.

Colorado Mining Directory and Buyers' Guide. Denver: G. A. Wahlgreen, 1901.

Encyclopedia of American Business History and Biography: Railroads in the Age of Regulation, 1900-1980. New York: Bruccoli Clark Layman, Inc., 1988.

Encyclopedia of American Business History and Biography: Railroads of the Nineteenth Century. New York: Bruccoli Clark Layman, Inc., 1988.

First Annual Colorado Mining Directory, 1896. Compiled by J. S. Bartow and P. A. Simmons. Denver: The Colorado Mining Directory Co.

Map of Colorado Territory, Embracing the Central Gold Region. Drawn by Frederick J. Ebert under direction of the Governor, Wm. Gilpin. Published by Jacob Monk, 1862.

Map of Public Surveys in Colorado Territory. Map to accompany report of the Surveyor General, 1866, (Issued by the General Land Office on Oct. 2, 1866.)

Map of the State of Colorado. Compiled from the official Records of the General Land Office, 1987. Compiled by A. F. Dinsmore. Revised and corrected for reissue by M. Hendges.

Map of the State of Colorado, 1885. Compiled from the official Records of the General Land Office, Compiled and drawn by M. Hendges.

Map of the Territory of Colorado Showing the Extent of the Public Surveys. Map to accompany the Annual Report for 1871. Compiled under the direction of the Surveyor General.

National Archives, Cartographic and Architectural Branch, Washington, D.C.

Nell's New Topographical and Township Map of the State of Colorado. Compiled from U.S. Government Surveys and other authentic Sources, 1881.

Nell's Map of Colorado, 1885. Chain and Hardy Co., Agent, Denver, 1885.

Nell's Map of Colorado, 1902. Hamilton and Kendrick, Agent, Denver, 1902.

Post Route Map of the State of Colorado showing post offices with the intermediate distances and mail routes in operation on the 1st of October, 1885.

Thayer's Map of Colorado Published by H. L. Thayer, Denver, Col., 1880. From Surveys of the General Land Office, used by permission, revised and corrected to date by the Publisher.

United States Geological Survey, Maps, U.S. Department of the Interior, Federal Center, Denver.

United States Department of Agriculture, Forest Service Maps, U.S. Forest Service, Denver.

Williams' Tourist's Map of Colorado and the San Juan Mines. Engraved from Surveys by the Hayden U.S. Geological Expedition. Henry W. Troy, Designer, N.Y., 1877.

Index